T0299586

AROUND THE WORLD IN 50 SLOPES

PATRICK THORNE

AROUND THE WORLD IN 50 SLOPES

WILDFIRE

First published in 2022 by
WILDFIRE
an imprint of HEADLINE PUBLISHING GROUP

3

Cataloguing in Publication Data is available from the British Library

Hardback ISBN 978 1 4722 9435 7

Map illustrations by Andrew Torrens

Typeset by EM&EN
Printed and bound in Great Britain by Clays Ltd, Elcograf S.p.A.

Headline's policy is to use papers that are natural, renewable and recyclable
products and made from wood grown in well-managed forests and other
controlled sources. The logging and manufacturing processes are expected
to conform to the environmental regulations of the country of origin.

HEADLINE PUBLISHING GROUP
An Hachette UK Company
Carmelite House
50 Victoria Embankment
London EC4Y 0DZ

The authorised representative in the EEA is Hachette Ireland, 8 Castlecourt
Centre, Dublin 15, D15 XTP3, Ireland (email: info@hbgi.ie)

www.headline.co.uk
www.hachette.co.uk

For Sally, Sam, Alexander and Robert

Contents

A Note on Sources and Run Order

The author has made every effort to verify the figures and measurements found in this book and, where available, has used official statistics. Resort staff and knowledgeable locals were asked to check stats at the respective slopes to verify as much information as possible. As skiers will know, however, different measurement systems are in use around the world and there is no global standard. As such, many figures are contestable, open to error and, in some cases, prone to change. For example, European ski areas typically measure slope length and number of runs whereas North America and most other countries list ski area size in hectares and acres. In each case the relevant official data has been included.

The 50 runs in this book are ordered to create a long and meandering circumnavigation of the globe through the world's most interesting ski slopes, ending with a Pacific crossing from New Zealand to California.

DAVE'S RUN, MAMMOTH MOUNTAIN

CALIFORNIA, USA

Dave and Roma McCoy built one of the world's great ski resorts from scratch. Over 70 years, Mammoth has grown into one of America's (and the planet's) biggest, covering 1,416+ hectares (3,500+ acres), with 175 separate ski runs. It's only fitting that one run, a high black diamond near the summit, is named after Dave.

Mammoth Mountain is a vast dormant volcano, a ski area 9.5 kilometres (6 miles) wide and the culmination of all Dave achieved. It's an answer to the early critics of his vision for Mammoth, who dismissed it as 'too remote' and 'too high'. This must have added to the satisfaction of finally building a lift up to the highest point of the mountain.

Dave and Roma met at a soda fountain in Independence, California, in the autumn of 1939, when he was 23, she 18. By this time McCoy, who made his first pair of skis as a school project, had already become the state's champion skier. Dave had also already set up one ski area, with a primitive lift made from parts of a Model 'A' Ford truck (not an unusual idea in those ski pioneering times). McCoy sought finance to build a permanent rope tow for his ski area and approached the bank where Roma was working for an $85 loan. The story goes that the bank initially said no, but Roma persuaded them to change their minds.

The pair were married on 10 May 1941 and spent their honeymoon at a remote cabin, which required skiing the 14.5 kilometres (9 miles) in. A year later Dave switched from his original ski area location to Mammoth, as he noted it had more reliable snow cover. The early years, indeed the early decades, were not easy. Dave sold his beloved Harley-Davidson to help finance the ski area and maintain the lift, and Roma collected the coins from ticket sales in a cigar box (these days a day pass will set you back more than $100). The base lodge at the time had a footprint of less than 32 square metres (340 square feet), an earth floor and an outdoor toilet. It wasn't until 1955 that the first chairlift, a second-hand model, was installed, and not until the early 1980s, after around four decades of hard labour by Dave and Roma, that Mammoth started to come into its own.

Being so high altitude, Mammoth has one of the longest and most reliable seasons in the world, usually starting in early November (sometimes, as in 2021, Halloween weekend in October) and quite often running through to the following summer. The resort receives an average of just over 10 metres (33 feet) of snowfall each year, one of the highest in North America and, indeed, the whole world, along with a whole lot of Californian sunshine. This means it sometimes offers skiing and boarding on US Independence Day, 4 July, and now and then right through to August. That's one of the longest ski seasons anywhere in the world (some years THE longest) for a ski area without a glacier. Dave, who worked as a hydrographer for the Los Angeles Department of Water and Power before finally being able to work full time on Mammoth, knew where the best snow was.

If you're travelling a long way to visit Mammoth, it's worth noting that the ski area is only a few dozen miles, as the crow flies, south-east of Yosemite National Park and its incredible giant sequoia trees. Unfortunately, the Tioga Pass between the two is blocked by snow in winter,

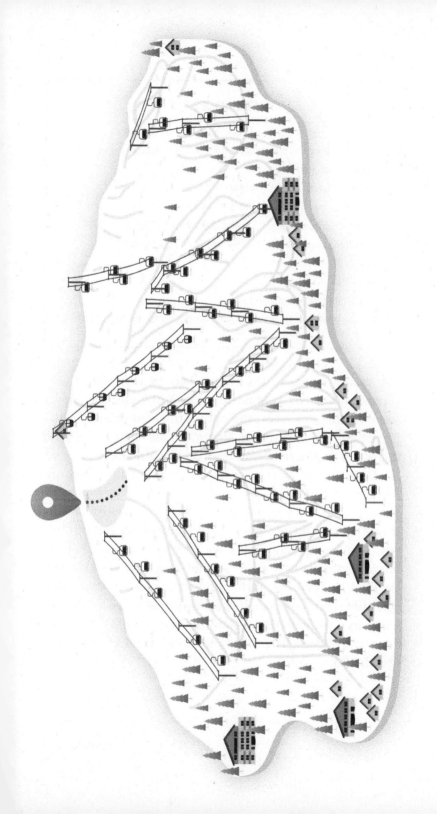

FACT FILE

IN SHORT A run at the top of one of the world's great ski areas,
dedicated to its founder who created it from nothing.

DIFFICULTY OF RUN Difficult

VERTICAL OF RUN 73 metres (240 feet)

LENGTH OF RUN 464 metres (1,522 feet)

SKI AREA ALTITUDE RANGE 2,424–3,369 metres (7,953–11,053 feet)

RESORT AREA DIMENSIONS 1,416+ hectares (3,500+ acres)

RUNS 175

LIFTS 25

WEB mammothmountain.com

GETTING THERE Air to Mammoth Yosemite, 19 kilometres (12 miles)

but usually opens at the end of May (it varies each year depending on the volume of snow to be cleared). Apart from visiting the trees, the option to swim or surf in the Pacific and ski or board at Mammoth also gets easier (and the ocean warmer) around that time of year.

Dave retired at the age of 90, having run Mammoth for almost 7 decades. He and Roma sold the resort for $365 million to a private investment firm. Dave and Roma stayed active all their lives. Dave kept skiing well into his 80s, then in his later years became particularly keen on photographing the nature around him that he so loved. He died in 2020, aged 104, and Roma died a year later, aged 100. They were married for nearly 80 years and raised 6 children while building Mammoth. As of 2021, they had 19 grandchildren, 34 great-grandchildren and 1 great-great-grandchild.

WARM SPRINGS, SUN VALLEY

IDAHO, USA

Ski touring – hiking up the slopes to freeride down – has had something of a renaissance in recent years, as skiers and boarders enjoy the freedom it allows. Yet I think most of us would still prefer to use a ski lift to get up the slopes.

As with all things ski history, there's some dispute over what constituted the first ski lift. Skiers used trains to get up slopes in the late nineteenth century, for example, but these were not built specifically for skiing. The top candidates were a series of essentially large sit-in sleds that were pulled uphill by a cable, each carrying four or more people, in the first decades of the twentieth century.

The very first of those cable-towed uphill sleds is believed to have been one in the German Black Forest, which started operating on Valentine's Day in 1908. Invented by a Robert Winterhalder, it ran on hydroelectricity. Now we've gone full circle, with more and more ski lifts around the world switching to green power.

The days of the 'uphill-cable-sled' lifts were numbered when early cable cars (known as trams in North America) began to appear in ski resorts in the late 1920s, followed by the first of the modern drag lifts (where you stand on your skis to be pulled up) at Davos in Switzerland in 1934. But the invention that really made ski holidays feel like, well, holidays, was the chairlift. The idea of being comfortably carried up the mountain, not needing to learn to balance as you were dragged, fitted the American Dream perfectly, and in the late 1930s the first chairlift appeared at Sun Valley in Idaho.

The story goes that in 1935, a gentleman with the wonderful name of Count Felix Schaffgotsch was tasked with finding the location for 'the perfect grand American ski resort' by Averell Harriman, then boss of the Union Pacific Railroad. Count Felix eventually settled on the mountains of the Wood River Valley around the old mining town of Ketchum, which he reported more delightful than the European Alps.

Harriman agreed but wanted more than the perfect location, and tasked James Curran of Union Pacific's engineering department with designing the lifts for his dream resort. Curran had previously worked on industrial overhead banana conveyor systems used to load cargo ships. He replaced the banana hooks with chairs and the world's first three ski chairlifts were installed in 1936 and 1937. The rest is history.

Sun Valley was an almost instant success and remains so to this day. Its status was secured when, in 1940, just a few years after those first chairlifts were installed, it hosted what's recorded as North America's first international ski race, the Harriman Cup, named after the founder. It's particularly associated with Hollywood A-listers, as well as famous writers, artists, industrialists, politicians and their ilk, past and present. Early guests included Errol Flynn, Ernest Hemingway, Clark Gable, Gary Cooper, Marilyn Monroe and Lucille Ball, along with several members of the Kennedy dynasty.

Sun Valley is a ski resort with great skiing for all abilities, but the run that is most admired as one of North America's best is Warm Springs, a steep run of 1,006 vertical metres (3,300 feet) that continues at a fairly constant pitch for around 3 kilometres (almost 2 miles). It's a real leg-burner.

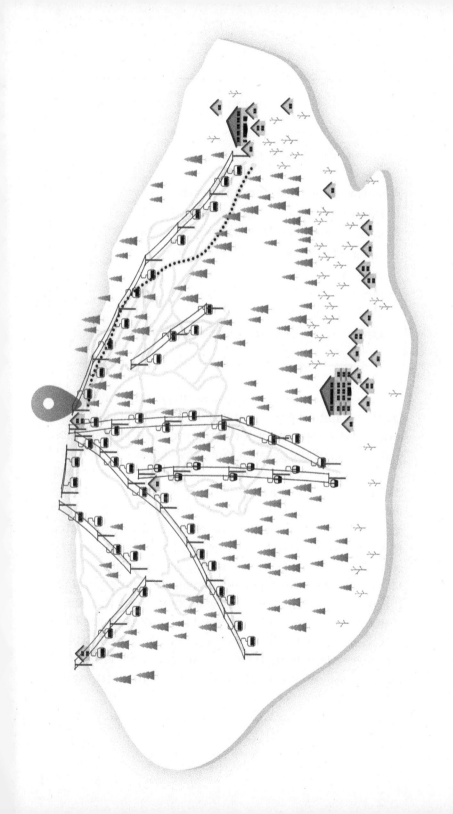

FACT FILE

IN SHORT One of the best ski runs in North America, and the ski
area that gave the world chairlifts.

DIFFICULTY OF RUN Moderate

VERTICAL OF RUN 1,006 metres (3,300 feet)

LENGTH OF RUN 3.6 kilometres (2 miles)

SKI AREA ALTITUDE RANGE 1,752–2,788 metres (5,748–9,150 feet)

RESORT AREA DIMENSIONS 971 hectares (2,400 acres)

RUNS 65

LIFTS 13

WEB sunvalley.com

GETTING THERE Air to Hailey's Friedman, 22 kilometres (14 miles)

Fans of the run, who include international ski racers, say that standard pitch, coupled with a north-facing orientation and a reputation for being groomed to perfection, make it one of the greatest runs anywhere.

Located above the Sun Valley suburb of Warm Springs, the wide run is accessed via either the Challenger, Christmas or Lookout Express quad chairlifts, the modern incarnations of those first chairlifts installed more than 85 years ago. Two of those three original chairlifts are long gone, but the last is still standing on Sun Valley's Ruud Mountain. It's worth paying homage to while you're in the resort, located along Fairway Road from the centre. Although chairlifts today have up to eight seats per chair, sometimes pull-down hoods, occasionally digital displays on their safety bars, even heated seats and Wi-Fi, with Porsche designing some to make them look extra stylish, you'll still note how little has changed in the basic design of the chairlift from that original patent.

Harriman's vision and Curran's lift design proved incredibly popular. In the golden age of Hollywood it was the go-to destination for numerous film stars, and many films were shot there. It remains one of the world's great resorts.

5 MILE, SUN PEAKS

BRITISH COLUMBIA, CANADA

Every skier wants something different from their holiday, so how do you go about creating the perfect ski resort? It's an impossible task. In fact, many ski areas become victims of their own success. Their popularity leads to them being over-developed and over-crowded. An escape to the open space of the mountains becomes the same battle it is on the streets. Plus a sizeable chunk of skiers want to stay in a small city at the base of the slopes with all the amenities that offers.

No one knows this better than husband and wife team Al and Nancy Greene Raine. Both were already famous in the ski racing world when they moved to Whistler, then an undeveloped backwater in the early 1970s. While raising a young family, they were instrumental in Whistler's growth into the world-leading resort it is today, with North America's largest ski area and a legacy that includes hosting the 2010 Winter Olympics.

But having done much of the work of persuading government and investors to back Whistler's development, and conceiving the ski area on Blackcomb Mountain, Al and Nancy moved on in the early 1990s, just as Whistler Blackcomb was making its debut on 'must ski before I die' lists.

Their destination was the rundown ski area of Tod Mountain, renamed Sun Peaks, some 350 kilometres (218 miles) to the east, close to the small city of Kamloops and right in the heart of British Columbia. The past three decades have seen Al, Nancy and team grow Sun Peaks to

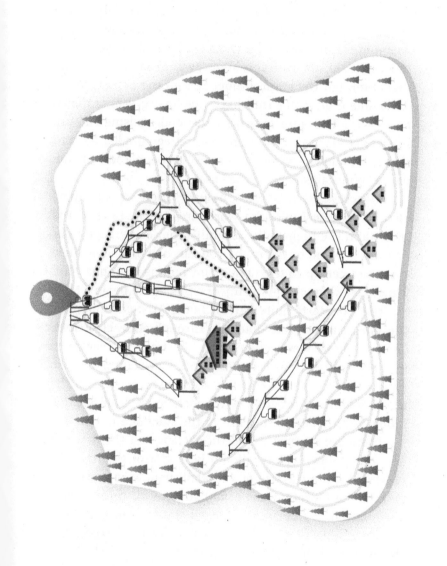

become Canada's second-largest ski area, with more than 1,700 hectares (4,200 acres) of terrain and 138 runs. Even so, the resort village remains relatively small, compact, intimate and friendly. It has the same user-friendly design as Whistler, thanks to the team at Ecosign, but the sense of a genuine local community is strong. Everything you need, especially ski lift access, is steps away from your accommodation, but the guest-to-slope-space ratio is perfection.

5 Mile is an iconic run that sums up everything that is Sun Peaks. The resort's longest run and utilising the full lift-served vertical, it's an epic easy green-graded descent that carves down through the forest between Tod and Sundance mountains back to the base.

To access it, take the Sunburst then Crystal quad chairlifts to the Top of the World area (at the peak of Tod Mountain, the highest lift summit) from the Village Base; or from one end of the resort you can hop on the Burfield quad and get up to the same point on one long quad lift. Turn skier's right from the top of either lift to begin 5 Mile.

The run starts quite narrow but gentle, cutting along the side of upper Tod Mountain through snow-clad trees. Then fabulous views open up to the right as black diamond terrain such as Rice Bowl and Pink Flamingos drop away on one side. As 5 Mile sweeps back around to the right, becoming progressively wider, another black diamond, White Rabbit, starts from the skier's left.

These are all enticing for future laps, but the first run of the day down 5 Mile should be a glorious cruise. The slope widens to the size of a football field as it passes the base of the Elevation chair, and runs of all types funnel down into it. It's perfect for mixed ability groups and lets the more able skiers take The Other Way to experience all kinds of little side ventures, including unmarked tree

FACT FILE

IN SHORT A marvellous cruise with many options from two of the great names in Canadian skiing.

DIFFICULTY OF RUN Easy

VERTICAL OF RUN 825 metres (2,707 feet)

LENGTH OF RUN 8 kilometres (5 miles)

SKI AREA ALTITUDE RANGE 1,255–2,152 metres (4,117–7,060 feet)

RESORT AREA DIMENSIONS 1,728 hectares (4,270 acres)

RUNS 138

LIFTS 13

WEB sunpeaksresort.com

GETTING THERE Rail to Kamloops, 52 kilometres (33 miles); or Air to Kamloops, 62 kilometres (38 miles)

runs. One, known to locals as 'Inner Child', is a line that includes some nice banked turns created by a summer mountain bike track.

Nancy's determination to make a success of Sun Peaks comes from a go-getting attitude that was bred into her at a young age. Her ski racing success was exceptional, winning the inaugural World Cup tour in 1967 and repeating the feat in 1968, breaking the European domination of the past. Jean-Claude Killy won the men's titles in the same years. Nancy also took two medals in the 1968 Winter Olympics, at Grenoble in France, including gold in the giant slalom by 2.68 seconds, still one of the biggest margins in Olympic ski racing history.

Despite retiring from racing aged 24, Nancy remains the most successful Canadian ski racer of all time, with cabinets full of glittering trophies in Cahilty Lodge, the

Sun Peaks accommodation she established with Al, who became the new municipality's mayor. If all this wasn't enough, Nancy also served as a Canadian Senator for BC, from 2009 until mandatory retirement, aged 75.

An important thing to note about Sun Peaks is that Al and Nancy have sought to build a community as much as a destination resort, battling to secure public funds to invest in facilities for the people who have moved to the area to make Sun Peaks their home. They've particularly focused on supporting the younger generation. One of the coolest examples of this is a small elementary school located at the top of the Village Platter lift where the local kids can ski-out at the end of the school day.

Nancy has long been Director of Skiing at Sun Peaks, and skis most days with any resort guests who want to come along, free of charge, meeting at 1pm at the top of the Sunburst Express chairlift.

Apart from the kudos of skiing with the lady who was, for good reason, named Canada's female athlete of the twentieth century, and enjoying some fabulous terrain, Nancy offers some of the best no-nonsense advice gleaned from her lifetime in the sport, including: 'Look ahead, not down, when you ski. You paid a lot of money for this holiday so look at the view, not at your feet.'

CPR RIDGE, KICKING HORSE

BRITISH COLUMBIA, CANADA

A good many famous (and less famous) North American ski areas owe their existence to the development of railways. Initially, pioneers surveyed routes through the mountains for the train lines, and supply points along the way grew into towns. Then railway employees or other settlers from snowy parts of Europe saw a nice snow-covered slope and thought they'd try hiking up and have a ski down. Often thought eccentric (occasionally bordering on insane) by their contemporaries, a century or so later some of those first ski runs are now part of billion-dollar resorts.

Of course, the railways didn't just have an impact on the development of ski resorts in North America. In the late nineteenth century and the start of the twentieth century, railways were under construction through mountains all over the world, and there was usually a skier or two among the workers involved who realised they could use the new train line as a ski lift, be it along the Argentina–Chile border, or even in countries like Iran.

Kicking Horse ski resort on the western side of British Columbia takes its name from the mountain pass it sits in, above the railway town of Golden. The kicking horse in question was owned by the surgeon and naturalist James Hector, a native of Edinburgh, Scotland. In 1858 Hector was employed as a doctor and naturalist on the Palliser Expedition, which was seeking to find a route for the railway through the Canadian Rockies. Chasing after his straying horse one day, Hector was kicked in the chest by it and thought dead by his workmates, who duly dug him a grave and were about to put him in it when he regained consciousness. The pass and river where this happened were named after the incident, and 142 years later in the year 2000, so was the ski resort.

Kicking Horse Mountain Resort (KHMR), to give it its full title, made quite a splash when it appeared. Located in an area famous for its light powder snow (they've trademarked 'Champagne Powder Capital of Canada'™), the Golden Eagle Express gondola climbs over 1,300 vertical metres (4,265 feet) from base to summit, one of the greatest and fastest vertical climbs by a single lift anywhere in the world, opening up what was then one of North America's five biggest lift-served verticals.

Although it has plenty of family-friendly slopes and some glorious long top-to-bottom cruises taking in marvellous views out across the pass below, the word that got out to serious skiers and boarders was about the abundance of 'steep and deep' terrain, and it soon started to draw skiers from around the planet in the same way that resorts such as Chamonix, St Anton and Niseko do. Now, Kicking Horse has the highest proportion of expert skiing of any resort in North America (60 per cent).

The huge Alpine bowls are the main attraction for this type of skier, and specifically the myriad of chutes that drop off the ridges above. There are now more than 85 named chutes, all graded steep black diamond or very steep double black diamond. They drop off ridges in sectors with suitably inspiring or alarming names (depending on your point of view), such as Terminator Peak, Whitewall and Redemption Ridge. Among the easiest to reach, a few metres from the top station of the gondola, is CPR Ridge, which accesses 16 double black diamond chutes. Its name

pays homage to the railway roots of the region – CPR is of course the Canadian Pacific Railway.

The rail references continue in the names of the 16 chutes – each with a rail theme, or a pun on one, such as chute 49, Local Motion. Or you can drop off CPR into double black diamond chutes 52 (Boxcar), 53 (Whistle Blower), 54 (Derail), 57 (Spurline), 58 (Main Line) . . . and so it goes on. The great thing is that it's easy to do loops and try each chute, as they all funnel down to the main top-to-bottom easy trail It's A Ten (10), from which you can cruise on down to the bottom of the gondola or jump off onto another blue or black diamond run further down the mountain. Alternatively, just cut across and jump on the Stairway To Heaven quad chair and drop into Feuz Bowl. Queues for gondola or chairlifts are a rarity, with an average day seeing just less than one skier/boarder

---

per acre of available terrain (there are 1,410 hectares/ 3,486 acres).

It's important to understand that these chutes are not for the unprepared. Many have a 45-degree pitch, some have a couple of metres of vertical off the top to drop into. While the locals bounce down effortlessly and know chutes that aren't even marked on the trail map, for the rest of us some nerve-building may be required before launching ourselves over the edge. The good news is that the chutes are filled with that abundant soft powder for which Kicking Horse is famous, so it's going to be a soft landing if you fall. But once you've conquered the nerves and mastered the quick turns needed on these gradients, you'll be bouncing off the edges of the chutes in no time, whooping with joy at the exhilaration of it all.

When you stop for a breather, you can take in the magnificent views out over the valley and perhaps catch sight of a train moving slowly along through Kicking Horse Pass below, thanks to the efforts of James Hector (and his horse) on the Palliser Expedition a century and a half ago.

ED'S RUN, WHITEFISH
MOUNTAIN RESORT

MONTANA, USA

Two men are credited with saying very similar things. The great Scottish-American naturalist John Muir said, 'I'd rather be in the mountains thinking of God, than in church thinking about the mountains,' while Norwegian explorer Fridtjof Nansen went with, 'It is better to go skiing and think of God, than go to church and think of sport.'

The point of both is, of course, what many of us who travel to the mountains find, that their scale and majesty tends to dwarf all human achievement. Whether we're religious or not, these awe-inspiring places remind us just how small our own place in the universe is.

The relationship between religion and ski resorts is everywhere, with most believers of all faiths giving particular significance to mountains, sometimes because they feel they bring them closer to God.

In the case of Christianity that's partly perhaps because the northern hemisphere's ski season runs from about when the Three Kings set off to follow the star, right through to Easter. You'll find crucifixes erected on many mountain peaks, while some resorts build chapels and churches in their areas. It's common for new ski lifts to be blessed by a priest before they enter service. There are Christian ski groups and ski holiday companies; mountain retreats exclusively for Christian skiers and snowboarders; and Christian charities set up to distribute unwanted skiwear to the poor in colder areas of the world.

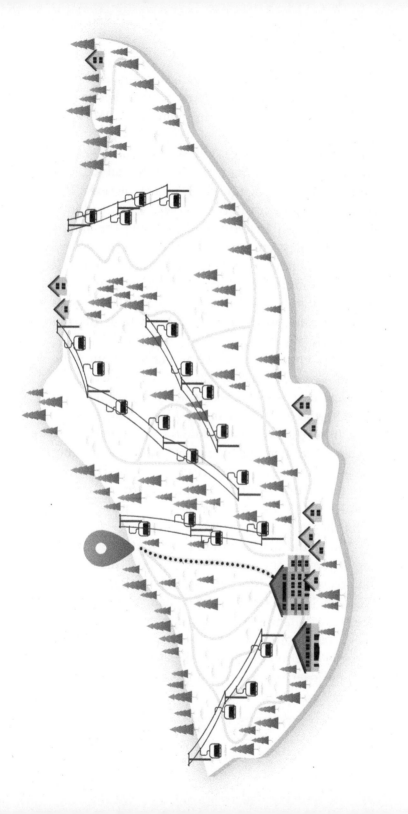

Big Mountain near Whitefish, Montana, is also home to Whitefish Mountain Resort. American soldiers of the 10th Mountain Division, returning home after World War II, inspired the local chapter of the Knights of Columbus to erect a six-feet-high statue of Jesus there in 1954, draped in a blue robe. (Ex-soldiers from the 10th Mountain Division were key players in the development of several leading ski areas in America in the post-war years, including Vail in Colorado.) In fact, the ski resort and the statue have completely separate permits from the US Forest Service to claim their place on the mountain. The ski resort doesn't own or maintain the statue, although you can ski right up to it. The statue actually stands on a plinth at least as high again, but due to the deep snow in winter the plinth is completely hidden.

Today known simply as the Big Mountain Jesus, he's become synonymous with the ski area, fondly regarded by believers and non-believers alike. It's perhaps the latter, though, who tend to enhance Big Mountain Jesus's appearance from time to time, adding a ski helmet, a fetching string of beads or a wig. And the Knights of Columbus say he sometimes need a fresh coat of paint and a little repair due to an unfortunate accident, when an enthusiastic boarder or freeskier has attempted to feature him in some stunt they're filming for social media.

You'll find Big Mountain Jesus waiting for you at the top of chair 2, the Swift Creek Express. This is one of the ski area's shorter lifts and, fittingly perhaps, serves some pleasant, benign terrain rather than the steeps for which the resort is famous. The statue is right beside the top of Ed's Run, an open, sometimes groomed but often slightly mogully blue-square-rated trail. Before you set off, you can gaze out over the resort and the majestic Flathead Valley

FACT FILE

IN SHORT A life-size statue of Jesus Christ above a Montana ski area has been dividing skier opinion for around 70 years.

DIFFICULTY OF RUN Moderate

VERTICAL OF RUN 338 metres (1,110 feet)

LENGTH OF RUN 1.6 kilometres (1 mile)

SKI AREA ALTITUDE RANGE 1,361–2,078 metres (4,464–6,817 feet)

RESORT AREA DIMENSIONS 1,214 hectares (3,000 acres)

RUNS 111

LIFTS 14

WEB skiwhitefish.com

GETTING THERE Rail to Whitefish Depot, 11 kilometres (7 miles); or Air to Glacier Park International, 30 kilometres (19 miles)

beyond, just as the Big Mountain Jesus is doing. Ed's Run is a joy to descend to the resort base below and keeps the view all the way down; it's also floodlit for night skiing.

One of the highest-profile 'religious skiers' (for want of a better term) was Pope John Paul II, who was a keen skier and lover of the mountains. There's now an annual race staged in his memory in the mountains of his home country of Poland: young priests dressed in heavy cassocks speed down the slopes, showing impressive skills despite the unusual ski garb. The Pope himself had a more conventional ski jacket, which made its way from the Vatican to a Roman Catholic High School named after him in Tennessee, USA, a state with just one ski area at Ober Gatlinburg in the Smoky Mountains. It is no longer worn on the slopes, however, and is reported to have pride of place in a glass display cabinet. Since John Paul II's death and subsequent beatification, the jacket is believed to have become a holy relic (second class) in the eyes of the Church.

For most of the twentieth century, Big Mountain Jesus stood on the slopes without knowingly upsetting anyone, but more recently 'freedom and liberty' groups launched legal challenges to his being there. The fact that Big Mountain Jesus is a statue of, well, Jesus, is at odds, they argue, with the First Amendment of the US Constitution, which specifically requires the separation of religion and state. The Jesus statue, as well as the ski slopes of Whitefish Mountain Resort, are both on publicly owned federal land.

In 2010, the Forest Service did initially accept that view and said its policy was to remove all 'memorials' from its land. It then changed its mind following a public outcry, deciding Big Mountain Jesus was 'a unique case'. After battles in court, the argument that the statue is a 'military memorial' and not wholly religious won the day, for now at least.

If you get split from your group, you know the spot to meet: 'See you at Big Mountain Jesus.'

FOREST MEADOW, LOVELAND

COLORADO, USA

Valentine's Day is a big deal in ski areas across the northern hemisphere, falling as it does in the middle of the
ski season. There are plenty of romance-themed events,
of course. Among the more popular are romantic meals
served in slow-moving gondola cabins after the day crowds
have departed. Chairlift speed-dating is another wide-
spread favourite. Those 'looking for love' line up in two
columns to board a double chairlift and have until the lift
reaches the top to decide whether they want to ski off into
the sunset together (or more likely the nearest mountain
restaurant) or instead ski off down different sides of the
mountain.

Loveland in Colorado, one of the world's highest-
altitude ski areas, lives up to its name by staging a mass
mountain-top wedding ceremony each Valentine's Day,
with the option for those already wed to renew their vows.
Established in the early 1990s, the annual 'Mountaintop
Matrimony' event has now been running for more than
three decades, each year seeing up to 100 couples tie
or retie the knot at high noon at a spectacular location
nearly 3,658 metres (12,000 feet) up on the Continental
Divide.

The event always makes newspaper headlines, if only
for the fabulous pictures of skiers and snowboarders,
some in full bridal attire, skiing down the slopes after the
ceremony. Couples wishing to be legally wed must be aged
over 18 and have a Colorado marriage licence ready; for
everyone else it's a blessing from the minister.

The wedding ceremony has occurred in different spectacular locations around Loveland's ski slopes over the years, but currently takes place on Forest Meadow, an easy green circle trail on beautiful forest-lined slopes. Happy-skiing-or-boarding-couples-to-be take triple Chair 2 from the base, then hop on to double Chair 6 up to the top of the treeline.

Off the chair it's a left turn on to Dealer's Choice, which runs a short way just above the treeline before merging into Forest Meadow. Then it's a lovely cruise down through an inspiring landscape of tall pines before it merges with another green circle trail, Turtle Creek, as it bends back to the base of Chair 6. It's a fabulous run to enjoy your first moment of marriage or renewed bliss.

If you want to take your love higher still, Loveland's Chair 9 is the second highest chairlift in Colorado, and indeed the world, reaching 3,871 metres (12,700 feet). There are two higher ski slopes in Europe and Asia, but at the top of Chair 9 are the world's fourth highest lift-accessed slopes. Most are steep single or double black diamond bowl skiing, but there is the Rookie Road if you prefer a gentler way down, or if you're still in your wedding dress.

Happy couples need to be able to ski back down the slope – there's no downhill transport for non-skiers. The resort also advises couples to beware of likely cold weather, as the ceremony takes place whatever the weather; it isn't cancelled unless the resort is in full stormbound closure, which is rare. In short – it's smart to wear thermals under your silk gown.

There is more to Loveland's annual ceremony than just the spectacular location. After the service, participants and their guests can join in the Honeymooners' Après

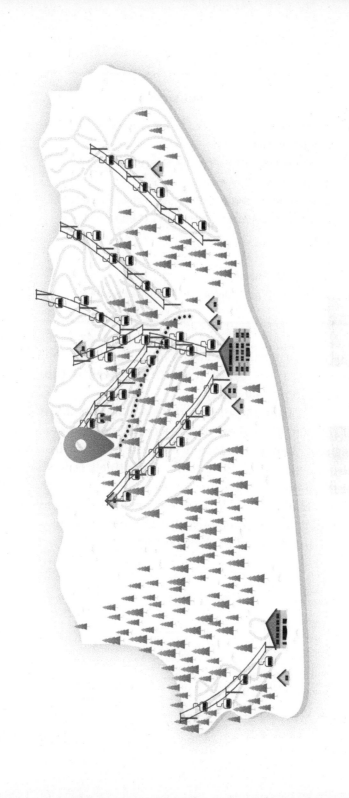

FACT FILE

IN SHORT A descent dedicated to true love like no other on earth.

DIFFICULTY OF RUN Easy

VERTICAL OF RUN 381 metres (1,250 feet)

LENGTH OF RUN 1.6 kilometres (1 mile)

SKI AREA ALTITUDE RANGE 3,292–3,966 metres (10,800–13,010 feet)

RESORT AREA DIMENSIONS 729 hectares (1,800 acres)

RUNS 94

LIFTS 11

WEB skiloveland.com

GETTING THERE Air to Denver, 74 kilometres (46 miles)

Party for a small fee. Rather than throwing confetti, or indeed rice, the resort requests bird seed is thrown for reasons of animal safety.

Apart from the all-important declaration of love at one of the planet's highest ski-lift-accessed points, couples who register their participation with the ski area in advance also receive a free lift pass for Valentine's Day when one of them buys a ticket. In fact, the official title of the event is the 'Marry Me & Ski for Free Valentine's Day Mountain-top Matrimony Ceremony'. What more enticing prospect could any suitor offer their betrothed?

PANDO, SKI COOPER

COLORADO, USA

Although the sport of snowboarding as we know it is not yet 50 years old, there's an ongoing debate about where it all began. The truth is that as with the even more protracted and still ongoing evolution of Alpine skiing, it has been a team effort.

If we ignore for the moment the depiction of something resembling snowboarders in a possibly 10,000-year-old cave painting in China, the consensus is that Sherman Poppen of Muskegon, Michigan, USA is the 'father of the snowboard'. He created a stand-on board he called the 'Snurfer' in 1965. Unlike the modern board, it needed no special footwear, no bindings, and you steered in part with a thin rope connected to the tip. Poppen produced the prototype from two waterskis bonded together. He's reported to have made it for his daughters, but ended up licensing the patent to a toy manufacturer which shifted around 750,000 of them over the following 15 years.

But rather like Mathias Zdarsky, prime candidate for 'the father of Alpine skiing' title who used one long ski pole to steer, akin to a Venetian gondolier, Poppen's version of a stand-on board is not what we think of as a snowboard today. Instead, snowboards, in something like their modern form, began to appear in the 1970s, with a few dedicated enthusiasts, often competitors in the various early Snurfer competitions, building prototype boards in their garages. They included Tom Sims of California's SIMS Snowboards (who would later stunt double for Roger Moore in an early snowboarding scene in the 1985 Bond film *A View to a Kill*), Chuck Barfoot, Chris Sanders, Jeff Grell, Mike Olson (who created Gnu Snowboards), and the name that has ended up dominating the global sport, Jake Burton.

But before Burton came to dominate, Dimitrije Milovich and Wayne Stoveken shone brightly in the mid-1970s with their patented 'Snow Surfboard', which they christened the 'Winterstick'. Some feel this was the first true snowboard, and it certainly made headlines across North America and was selling in 11 countries by 1975.

The big problem Winterstick and the other early snowboard companies faced was resistance from ski resorts. Most refused to let boarders on their slopes, particularly their lifts. Boarders usually had to practise their sport in state parks and other public hills. Winterstick ultimately failed, but others battled on, persuading smaller ski areas to let snowboards on their slopes.

Ski Cooper was one of the first: Richard Christiansen, a surf shop owner in Boulder, Colorado, recounts how he was intrigued when a man came in with a board saying he was using it on the snow. Christiansen called around Colorado's resorts asking if any would allow boarders on their slopes. All said no except Ski Cooper, whose owners were regulars at Christiansen's store.

When the day finally came, boarders descended on Ski Cooper from the East and West Coasts to compete for the title of 'King of the Mountain'. Little seems to be recorded of that initial competition over four decades ago – certainly Ski Cooper makes no reference to its crucial part in the sport's development. The resort highlights the fact that it 'does not overgroom its slopes creating hard packed surfaces as most ski areas do', and instead leaves things a little more natural, something that should suit

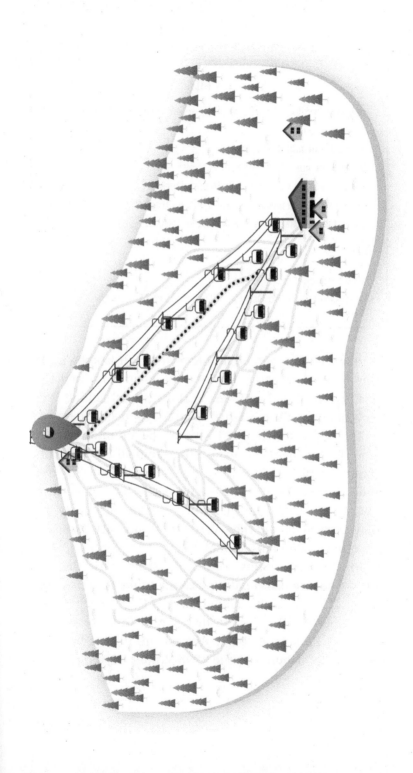

FACT FILE

IN SHORT A rewarding run at a key resort in the history of snowboarding.

DIFFICULTY OF RUN Difficult

VERTICAL OF RUN 301 metres (987 feet)

LENGTH OF RUN 1.5 kilometres (4,921 feet)

SKI AREA ALTITUDE RANGE 3,206–3,583 metres (10,520–11,757 feet)

RESORT AREA DIMENSIONS 194 hectares (480 acres)

RUNS 64

LIFTS 5

WEB skicooper.com

GETTING THERE Air to Denver, 210 kilometres (131 miles)

freeriders of all types, including boarders. It is known that some jumps were created down the main slope and that Sims placed second and Burton third overall behind Scott Jacobson, one of the original Winterstick team riders.

The year after the 1981 King of the Mountain competition, Burton helped organise the National Snow Surfing Championships at the little resort of Suicide Six near Woodstock in Vermont, his home state. That competition, now the US Open Snowboarding Championship, is still going, staged at another Vermont resort, Stratton, and attracting 30,000 fans annually.

In 1983 Tom Sims went one bigger with the first World Championship halfpipe competition staged at Soda Springs, California, his home state. By then snowboarding was going global, and the first World Cup contest was staged in Zürs in Arlberg, Austria, in 1985, before the sport finally debuted at the 1998 Winter Olympic Games in Nagano, Japan. That delay between the sport becoming mainstream and being introduced to the Olympics mirrors the early years of downhill skiing, which wasn't included in the first three Winter Olympic Games in the 1920s and 1930s.

But was the ever-higher standard the beginning of the end for the soul of the sport? Coming from skateboarding and surfing culture back in the 1980s and 1990s, some argued boarding wasn't about competition but camaraderie. In essence, trying to go one better than your fellow boarders just wasn't cool.

As snowboarding grew in popularity worldwide (at one point in the 1990s it was believed to be on a trajectory to overtake skiing), the many resorts that initially refused snowboarders access to their lifts and slopes had to quickly backtrack. Among those who left it late was Park City, Utah, now the biggest resort in the US, which only allowed boarders on its slopes shortly before it hosted snowboarding events at the 2002 Winter Olympics.

At the time of writing only three North American ski areas still ban boarders: Park City's neighbours Alta and Deer Valley in Utah, along with Mad River Glen in Vermont.

TEMPEST, SUNRISE PARK

ARIZONA, USA

In the twenty-first century, many governments in the Americas as well as Australia and New Zealand are finally putting human decency and justice first in their treatment of indigenous people. Several resorts, including North America's largest, Whistler, seek to engage with local tribes, in its case Squamish Nation and Lil'wat Nation, who maintain a cultural centre in the resort. Another in California, formerly known as Squaw Valley, is world-famous for many reasons, including hosting the 1960 Winter Olympics, the opening ceremony masterminded by Walt Disney. In 2021, it changed its name to Palisades Tahoe, deciding the former title was a 'a racist and sexist slur'.

Elsewhere, a bitter legal battle took place over the best part of 20 years at the Arizona Snowbowl ski area, where environmental groups and the local Navajo along with 12 other tribes all fought the resort's plans to use treated waste water for snowmaking. Ironically, resorts in other mountain regions where water is a particularly precious resource, such as Australia, have won 'eco awards' for this practice. In Arizona, the resort, which eventually won, argued that the purified waste water was cleaner than tap water. The tribes argued that they didn't care about that; to them it was disrespectful to spray effluent onto their sacred mountain.

There are some ski areas where the indigenous population have created the resort themselves. On 11 July 2020, the Batea Mahuida Snow Park opened to the world on a volcano in Patagonia, about 1,500 kilometres (930 miles)

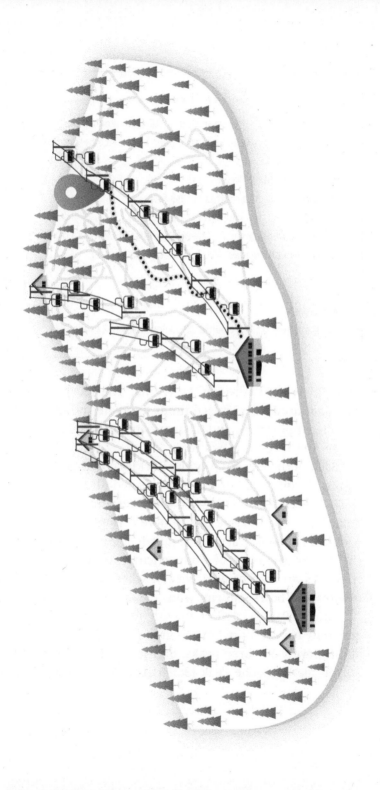

FACT FILE

IN SHORT A great run on land that is still managed by the indigenous people who have been here since before time immemorial.

DIFFICULTY OF RUN Difficult

VERTICAL OF RUN 330 metres (1,083 feet)

LENGTH OF RUN 1.95 kilometres (1.21 miles))

SKI AREA ALTITUDE RANGE 2,800–3,400 metres (9,200–11,100 feet)

RESORT AREA DIMENSIONS 486 hectares (1,200 acres)

RUNS 65

LIFTS 7

WEB sunrise.ski

GETTING THERE Air to Phoenix, 355 kilometres (221 miles)

south of Buenos Aires in Argentina. The local Mapuche Puel community had raised funds to create the ski area to provide employment and to stem depopulation, much like in the Alps a century before.

Back in the Eastern Arizona Rockies (also known as the White Mountains), Sunrise Park opened all the way back in December 1970. It's owned and operated by the White Mountain Apache Tribe in a remote corner of the 673,750 hectares (1,664,872 acres) – equivalent to more than half the size of the state of Connecticut – controlled by the tribe. It's an area of wild beauty, where mountain lions, coyotes and bears still run wild.

Sunrise Park started small with just a couple of lifts and generally easy terrain, but has grown to offer skiing for all ability levels on three peaks: Sunrise Peak (3,261 metres/ 10,700 feet), Apache Peak (3,383 metres/11,100 feet) and

Cyclone Circle (3,261 metres/10,700 feet). Early reviews in the ski press from 50 years ago demonstrate cynicism as to the likelihood of it succeeding, not to mention more casual racism.

The most challenging of the three peaks is Cyclone Circle, home to the majority of Sunrise Park's advanced terrain. The 16 runs here include several short, sharp double black diamond descents with such suitably descriptive titles as Thunder and Suicide. However, for a longer and hopefully more satisfying descent, as you ponder what it is to be skiing on a mountain still owned by the same people whose ancestors lived here long before Christopher Columbus left Spain, you need to ski Tempest.

It is the only black diamond run descending the full vertical of Cyclone Circle. At most resorts the high altitude would mean the slopes would be bare of vegetation, but here, thanks to the typically warmer weather at this more southerly latitude, there's thick pine forest lining the slopes right to the summit.

Standing at the top, Tempest appears as a white strip of ground dropping away steeply below you. It's unlikely Tempest will have been groomed, so how fresh the snow is will dictate the level of challenge. Actually, despite that southerly location and reputation for Arizona sunshine, Sunrise Park has an average of 635 centimetres (250 inches) of snowfall each season, so the chances are it will be fresh.

Apache Peak, the ski area's highest point, offers the best view from Apache Lodge, the highest ski lodge and restaurant in Arizona, from which New Mexico is visible on a clear day – as most days are. Given that this whole mountain is only served by a couple of nine-seat snowcats, it's also pretty likely you'll hardly see a soul as you make your descent. Skiing doesn't get much better than that.

33 CURÉ DESLAURIERS, MONT-TREMBLANT

QUEBEC, CANADA

Many ski resorts have been born where formerly prosperous ways of life are no longer viable, such as ex-mining towns or health spa resorts, or in agricultural communities left behind by modernisation and the general drift of rural populations to the cities. As a result, areas were often suffering population decline before wintersports were introduced to provide livelihoods. Some former ghost towns, where you couldn't give land away, are now famous resorts where a plot of land can cost a staggering amount.

In France, a national plan detailed the creation of many of the world's largest and greatest ski areas in the years after World War II. More often, however, the transformation comes down to the determination of just one or two people who love where they live and want to see the place thrive.

In Quebec, Canada, the success of eastern North America's most popular ski resort, Mont-Tremblant, can be attributed in large part to the arrival of Curé (Father) Charles-Hector Deslauriers, the community's first parish priest. The resort now has a ski run, number 33, named after him.

Arriving in the Upper Laurentians on 21 July 1929, Curé Deslauriers found something of a wasteland. With much of the mighty forest razed to the ground and the trees gone, there was little work remaining for the locals who had stayed. If he'd had hopes of restoring the community, his timing wasn't great. The Wall Street Crash

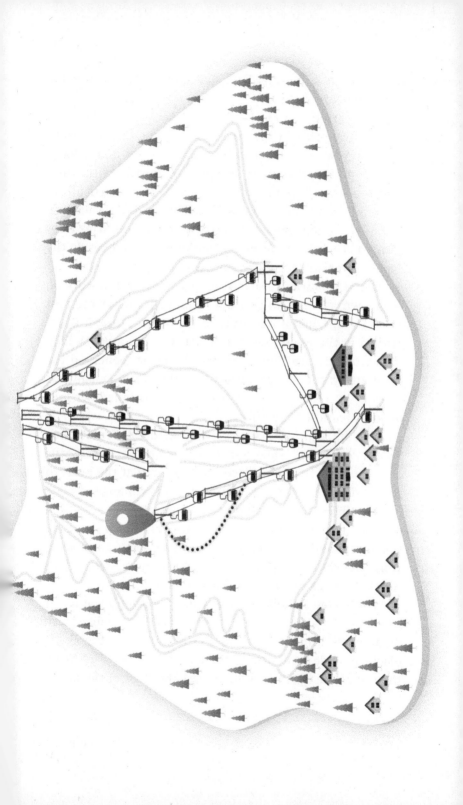

occurred three months later, with the Great Depression following close behind.

Undeterred, Curé Deslauriers set about building community pride in the area, starting one of the world's first reforestation efforts with tree planting and a focus on encouraging younger people to engage with their environment. He founded the Société d'horticulture de Mont-Tremblant and the Association de la vallée de la Rouge, organisations devoted to his cause. The trees planted are today most visible on Montée Ryan beside the Diable River and the golf courses.

Curé Deslauriers also encouraged the locals to work on their own gardens, organising a competition for the best kept. Then, when a rich American investor, Joseph Ryan, arrived in the region seeking to set up a ski area, Deslauriers worked with him to ensure the resort benefited the community. After Ryan's death, in 1950, Curé Deslauriers worked with Ryan's widow, Mary, who continued her husband's dream for Tremblant.

Run 33 Curé Deslauriers is located on Tremblant's *Versant Sud* (south side) and accessed by the Flying Mile quad chairlift from the Place Saint-Bernard at the heart of the modern resort, today famous for its brilliant redesign. In the 1990s, resort designers Ecosign created a style of pedestrianised slopeside village that pays homage to traditional regional architecture while integrating all modern conveniences, a concept since copied by resorts across North America and exported to the Alps.

The Flying Mile lift whisks you up through the forest loved by the Curé, passing rather alarming double black diamond terrain falling away to the right, and the single black Ligne de Pente run to the left. Turn skier's left from the top of the quad though, go past the start of the black,

FACT FILE

IN SHORT A run dedicated to a man who believed in a community when it had nothing, so that today it's one of the world's great resorts.

DIFFICULTY OF RUN Moderate

VERTICAL OF RUN 165 metres (541 feet)

LENGTH OF RUN 591 metres (1,939 feet)

SKI AREA ALTITUDE RANGE 230–875 metres (755–2,870 feet)

RESORT AREA DIMENSIONS 305 hectares (754 acres)

RUNS 102

LIFTS 14

WEB www.tremblant.ca

GETTING THERE Rail to Montreal, 132km (82 miles); or Air to Montreal, 125 kilometres (78 miles)

and the next descent you'll find is the much more mellow blue run 33. This carves around the mountain face and ends midway along the line of the quad. If you want to keep it blue, ski under and join run 29 Johannsen back down to the base.

The run also follows the line of the resort's Adrenaline Snowpark, where you can watch the young skiers and boarders of Tremblant who have stayed in the area thanks to the efforts of Curé Deslauriers and the Ryans that began nearly a century ago.

There are plenty of tales of how Curé Deslauriers connected the spiritual well-being of his parishioners to their love of skiing. One former choir boy, Peter Duncan, tells of how he was reluctant to commit to the choir given that it meant him losing weekend time on the slopes, but the

Curé won him over by allowing him to wear his ski boots under his cassock so that he could get onto the slopes faster after the service. Curé Deslauriers also organised a 'blessing of the skis' service at the start of each winter and ski days for village children several times a season.

Curé Deslauriers died on 23 April 1979, at the age of 81, having dedicated more than 50 years of his life to the people of Mont-Tremblant and seen his community grow into a world-class ski area. Besides the run, several other places around the resort are named after him, including a road and the lakeside Parc du Curé Deslauriers.

The process of fighting depopulation using ski resort development is still going on today, and new ski resorts are proposed in areas like Western Canada as developers hope to create 'the next Whistler'.

In Spain, the ski area of Cerler was established in the early 1970s and has seen the local population almost double over the past 25 years, from around 1,200 to nearly 2,200. The Aramón Group, which runs the ski lift, expanded into a third valley, Castanesa, to create what is now one of the country's largest ski areas. The local population of nearby Montanuy had seen population decline from just over 320 in the mid 1950s to nearer 200 in 2020. Montanuy now provides access to Cerler via the Castanesa Valley, and the hope is that the ski area's expansion will lead to population regrowth, just as it did with Tremblant a century ago. Time will tell.

LA FANTAISIE, MONT SUTTON

QUEBEC, CANADA

Resorts are always looking for the next trend to offer their skiers and boarders. Terrain park (and more briefly halfpipes) became a must-have from the early 1990s, and the conveyor lifts that hardly existed last century have multiplied in their thousands to make learning easier for skiers around the world.

At the start of the twenty-first century, 'glades' became a feature of every North American ski area worth its salt. 'Glade skiing' refers to a ski slope with trees to carve your turns around. This isn't what is commonly termed 'tree skiing' – off the piste through tightly packed natural forest – but usually a much gentler cruise between nicely spaced trees. There should be no low-lying branches or roots to be found just under the snow that you might catch your ski or board on as you descend.

These days, most moderate to large Canadian and US resorts have at least one gladed ski run, but it has dropped down the list of new season announcements. Instead, the current focus is back to off-piste skiing, now rebranded freeriding, with particular interest in 'earning your turns' by ski touring and hiking up.

Some ski areas stick to their strengths even when the latest fashion has moved on. Step forward Mont Sutton in the Eastern Townships of Quebec, down by the US border. Here, glade skiing has been the resort's big attraction since it opened in 1960. Except it's not called glade skiing. For one thing, despite the proximity to the state of Vermont less than five miles to the south, this is French-speaking

Quebec, so a 'mount' is a '*mont*' and 'glade skiing' is '*sous bois*' (literally 'undergrowth') skiing.

You might first realise that things are a little different here when you study the trail map. Most ski areas count the number of runs, Mont Sutton instead counts 'junctions' . . . and there are more than 200 of them. OK, they count runs too, there are 60 of them, and 45 per cent of the mountain's terrain is gladed. Those junctions, where the runs cross in the glades, give a nearly infinite number of combinations of descent. Start on one run, switch at the first junction, continue on another, switch at another. Talk about endless variety. Of course, you can just ski straight down without taking a turning at a junction if you really want to be radical.

La Fantaisie is the epitome of all that is great about glade skiing, and indeed Mont Sutton. Whether you call this a glade skiing trail or prefer the name tree skiing, it's a beautiful descent through a Golden Birch tree forest that offers fabulous sunset views. The trees are wide enough apart for sweeping snowboarding turns and it is testimony to its popularity that people still choose to ski it even though there is a 1.4 kilometre (just under a mile) flat ski-out from the base.

La Fantaisie is one of Sutton's steepest double-black-diamond-rated runs and the last of three that drop off to skier's right from blue run number 1: Alleghanys. You can reach it either by taking quad chairlift II from the mountain's main base at 400 metres (1,310 feet) altitude, then skiing down to one of the four chairlifts that serve the upper mountain, or you can skip the base of the mountain altogether and take the road up to the resort's second, higher base at 520 metres (1,700 feet), where you can jump

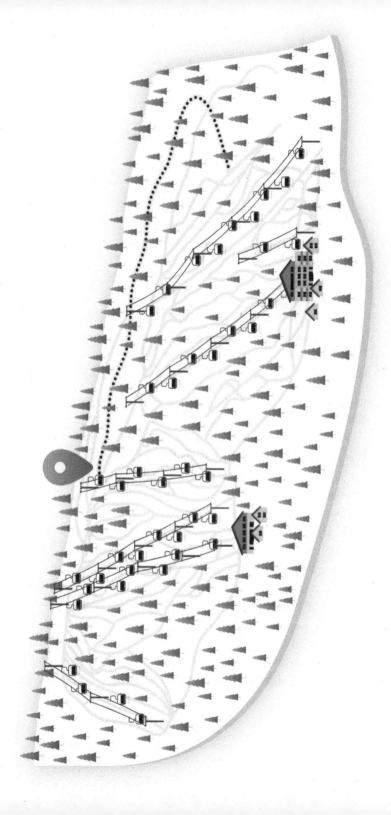

FACT FILE

IN SHORT A magical descent through the forest that epitomises a
ski area famed for its glades.

DIFFICULTY OF RUN Expert

VERTICAL OF RUN 440 metres (1,444 feet)

LENGTH OF RUN 1.6 kilometres (1 mile)

SKI AREA ALTITUDE RANGE 400–856 metres (1,310–2,808 feet)

RESORT AREA DIMENSIONS 93 hectares (230 acres)

RUNS 60 (& 204 junctions)

LIFTS 10

WEB montsutton.com

GETTING THERE Rail to Montreal, 122km (76 miles); or Air to
Montreal 128 kilometres (80 miles)

straight onto one of the chairs that take you up to run 1.
Plenty of pushing is required!

The run itself is simply a glorious steep and deep trail
through the forest, always at its best after fresh snowfall of
course, but lots of fun even when the snow is beaten down
by skiers before you. There are so many trees, so many
routes you can take between them, the tracks you can
make are almost as varied here as on the whole mountain.

The resort has taken the mountain into their hearts
– they always use the natural terrain rather than have
heavy machinery smooth paths through, making the most
of what Mother Nature provides. They also plant up to a
thousand more trees each year to give her a hand and
maintain the forest.

The town of Sutton, 5 kilometres (3 miles) to the west
of the mountain, was originally a French Canadian (or

Canadien) settlement. The community grew at the very end of the eighteenth century when Americans who had fought on the side of the British in the American Revolution settled there, just over the border. For some time there were more English speakers than French, although that's now tipped back to predominantly French. There were other minorities too, including a large contingent of German-speaking Swiss. All these cultures, often bringing different religions with them, somehow managed to get on just fine, on the whole, and Sutton is very peaceable and friendly. The small town is a lovely place to spend a ski holiday, with good shopping and some fabulous restaurants. It has an authentic, honest feel, very different to the corporate-run resorts.

LONG JOHN, MOUNT SNOW

VERMONT, USA

Only a handful of countries in Europe don't have at least one small drag lift to serve a high slope. Several of these – tiny states like the Vatican, San Marino and Monaco – are no surprise. More surprising are some of the countries that do offer skiing – southerly Cyprus with the Troodos Mountains, famously warm Portugal, or tiny Liechtenstein, for example, to which Prince Charles whisked the young Lady Diana to teach her to ski before their wedding, away from the hordes of paparazzi stationed at the usual British royal ski destination of Klosters in Switzerland.

When it comes to northern Europe, almost every country has a snow slope. Denmark had several even before it built a year-round dry slope on the site of a power station, and the famously flat Netherlands perhaps cheated a little by building half-a-dozen indoor snow centres, although they do include one of the world's biggest.

It's only the island of Ireland that doesn't have any lifts on its mountains. Of course, there have been ski ventures over the years of one kind or another. In the 1990s, a farmer offered skiers rides up Crockmore Mountain (526 metres/1,726 feet) in the Sperrin mountain range on the back of his tractor when there was snow, which of course was more common then than it is now. You can still ski in Ireland on dry ski slopes which have operated for the best part of five decades, with the Ski Club of Ireland running a slope at Kilternan in County Dublin, or there's the Craigavon dry slope in Northern Ireland.

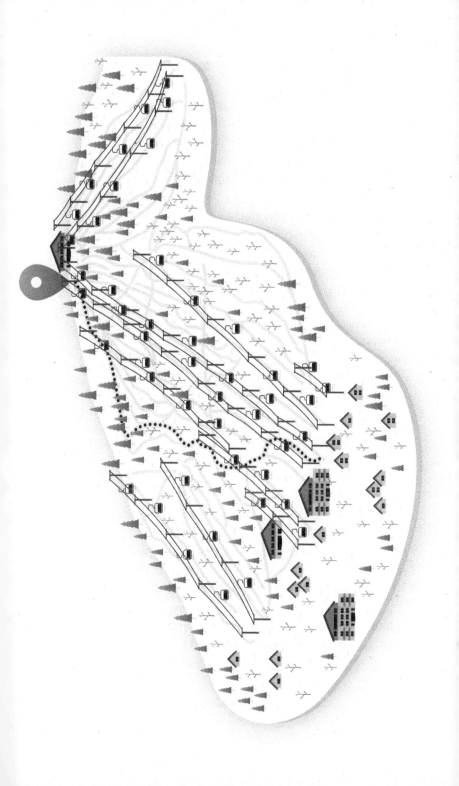

But despite (or perhaps because of) the lack of oppor-tunities to ski at home, the Irish have made a huge contribution to skiing worldwide, particularly après-ski-ing. The atmosphere of an Irish pub is perfectly in tune with the euphoria of an après-ski bar, so it is no surprise that hundreds exist in ski resorts from Andorra to Japan. Several Irish venues in Val Thorens, France, will even serve you what's claimed to be 'the highest Guinness in Europe'.

Irish nationals can also be found working in or some-times owning businesses in ski resorts across Europe and North America. Brexit gave a big boost to Irish people wanting to work in the Alps, as after Britain voted to limit the freedom of movement of its population, including their right to work in the EU, thousands of young Irish people stepped into the gap to work for holiday companies in the Alps.

Ireland's national day, St Patrick's, falls towards the end of the northern hemisphere's ski season when spirits are already high. St Paddy's Day on the slopes is celebrated the world over, although nowhere more so than in the US, particularly the East Coast.

There's a battle between ski areas to attract the lion's share of the St Patrick's Day market. Tempting offers include $17 lift tickets (to mark 17 March), treasure hunts in the snow for the proverbial 'pot 'o gold', Irish bands, and even scrambled eggs dyed green for breakfast and a simi-lar treatment to the après-ski beers. It's probably how the famous saint would want to have been celebrated.

Vermont's Mount Snow had probably the biggest St Patrick's Day gathering in recent years, reporting up to 10,000 celebrating on their slopes, many dressed in green. It's the easiest resort to reach from the US Northeast's met-ropolitan areas, so that figures. Celebrations are focused on

FACT FILE

IN SHORT A long green run in the Green Mountains of Vermont is the perfect run on which to celebrate all things Irish on St Patrick's Day.

DIFFICULTY OF RUN Easy

VERTICAL OF RUN 700 metres (2,297 feet)

LENGTH OF RUN 4.8 kilometres (almost 3 miles)

SKI AREA ALTITUDE RANGE 579–1,097 metres (1,900–3,600 feet)

RESORT AREA DIMENSIONS 243 hectares (601 acres)

RUNS 86

LIFTS 20

WEB mountsnow.com

GETTING THERE Rail to Brattleboro, 40 kilometres (25 miles); or Air to Boston, 216 kilometres (135 miles)

the resort's base lodge, where the green eggs are served and live bands play, but as the resort is located in Vermont's Green Mountains, with plenty of green circle runs to enjoy, it's worth making the most of that $17 lift ticket.

Long John is one of the resort's longest runs, winding down the mountainside above the base area from the summit. Accessible via several fast chairs including the Bluebird Express and Grand Summit Express lifts, turn left at the top and settle in for a lovely long cruise down the mountain. This whole run is designated a 'slow zone', so more experienced skiers and boarders can ride alongside those just starting to develop a love of the sport. Feel free to wish everyone you meet all the luck of the Irish.

Although Mount Snow and other resorts across New England step up to the plate come St Patrick's day (some have even been known to offer 'St Practice Day' a week before the 17th to build up to the annual event), what was the world's most Irish ski resort is, alas, no more.

Located in the Taconic Mountains of north-western Massachusetts, Brodie ski area opened in 1964 with an Irish theme, including runs named Shamrock and JFK. It was the brainchild of Jim Kelly, which was why the resort was nicknamed 'Kelly's Irish Alps'. The resort was known for its fun atmosphere, on the slopes (which on St Patrick's Days were famously dyed green) and off. While other ski areas had fairly basic base lodges at the time, which closed at dusk, Kelly built a three-storey lodge with carpeted floors topped with the huge Blarney Room. St. Patrick's Day at Brodie became 'St Patrick's Week' and actually extended to 10 days, incorporating the Irish Olympics and seeing the après-ski beers dyed green.

Senator Ted Kennedy was reputed to be a frequent visitor through to the 1980s, apparently enjoying the opportunity to spend a day in a relaxed spot where he could be himself. Unfortunately, Kelly's Irish Alps went the way of many small, family-run ski hills in the late twentieth century, losing out to corporate-run ventures. Jim sold up in 1999 and Brodie closed a few years later.

VOLCANO DESCENT, VILLARRICA

PUCÓN, CHILE

We have ancient seismic activity to thank for several of the world's great ski destinations. However, not content with dormant volcanoes, several ski lifts have gone up on the slopes of the 1,350 potentially active volcanoes worldwide. You can, if you wish, ski on the winter snow that coats gently vibrating, sometimes smoking volcanoes in New Zealand, Japan, Russia, and even in Europe, both up north in Iceland or down south in Sicily.

Arguably the most active volcano you can ski on is Chile's Volcan Villarrica, close to the small, pretty town of Pucón. Rated the most active volcano in Chile (a country in which the ski season at one resort or another is quite often interrupted by volcanic ash storms turning the snow grey), this vast stratovolcano towers almost a vertical mile (1,575 metres/5,170 feet) above the surrounding Southern Lakes region, 750 kilometres (465 miles) south of capital Santiago.

Scientists have worked out that this is at least the third Villarrica volcano to stand on this spot thanks to the violent seismic activity over past aeons. By coincidence, the ski area that exists here today is also the third. Only the first ski area was lost due to volcanic activity however; its replacement was not a successful business venture, but the third has thankfully got it right.

The current centre only dates to the late 1980s, making it one of the world's, and especially South America's, youngest resorts. Alas, not much has been updated since, so the four double chairlifts, which were already

---

second-hand when they were installed more than three decades ago, are getting rather elderly. The lower lifts serve the easiest terrain, which fortunately appeals to most of the clientele as the upper lifts are reported to be frequently out of action.

In any case, the run involves some hiking right up to the rim of the volcano for a truly unique ski descent. As with most classically shaped volcanos, the slope gets steeper as you climb higher. It's another 740 vertical metres (2,428 feet) from the top station of the highest lift at Piedra Negra to the smoking crater rim at 2,840 metres (9,317 feet). At best that's a two-hour hike, but (as mentioned) that top lift is rarely working, so you may have to start hiking lower down. Keep in mind the sometimes overpowering sulphurous odour and that increasing gradient. The volcano has a reputation for some of the deepest snow in South America, up to 12 metres (39 feet) towards the summit in a good year. To complicate things even further, it has a reputation for bad weather – cloud, gale-force winds and, of course, endless snowfall. Crampons will be required, which can be hired in Pucón. In short, you need to be fit, a very good skier and have the services of a local guide and full backcountry kit. For the best experience, you also need to get lucky with the weather.

If this all falls into place, your reward is a descent like no other, beginning with a peek over the rim to the bubbling magma below. Then look outwards for incredible views across southern South America. It's a truly world-class descent, 1,600 vertical metres (5,250 feet), the upper half all freeriding terrain; your guide should be able to lead you to some interesting lines created by former lava flows. Back down at ski area level you can join the marked trails, with a choice that includes some steep single and

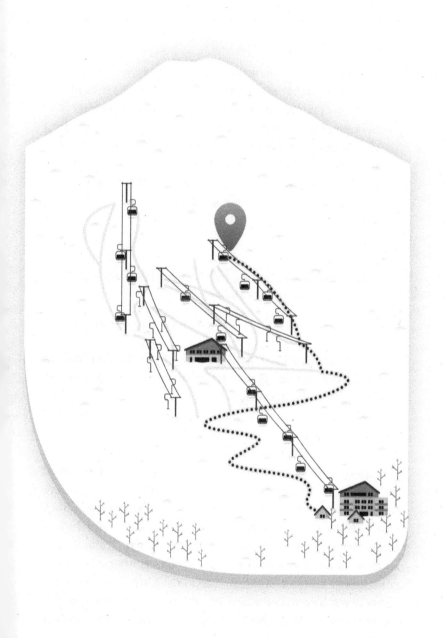

double black diamond runs in the upper section, easing
to intermediate then gentle trails down to the base as the
pitch of the slope decreases.

Villarrica (the name means 'place of wealth' and
comes from the Spanish conquests of the mid-sixteenth
century when silver and gold were mined here) has several
unusual features. Firstly, the current ski lifts are located
on north-facing slopes when most southern hemisphere
ski areas face south to get and hold the best snow. Villarrica's south face, though, is heavily glaciated and full of
large crevasses so isn't good for skiing, but fortunately the
volcano normally gets so much snow it still has one of the
continent's longest seasons. Secondly, the chairlifts have
rubber sections built into the towers to absorb the frequent rumblings of the mountainside. Avalanche danger

is normally low however, and volcanic ash clouds usually blow away from the slopes and Pucón itself.

Lakeside Pucón is one of Chile's leading year-round tourist destinations, with plenty of leisure activities on offer besides snow sports. The volcano towers above, a little like the Matterhorn above Zermatt, but here there's sometimes smoke emanating from the top and at night time an orange glow.

If you decide that skiing active volcanoes is for you, there are some other good options. Another Chilean ski area, Ski La Burbuja, sits on the famous Osorno volcano, which erupted 11 times between 1575 and 1869, including in 1835, when Charles Darwin spotted it as he sailed past in the *Beagle*.

Mount Etna has two ski centres, on the north and south side of the volcano. Lifts here have been 'taken out' by flying volcanic boulders at various times and had to be rebuilt. However, the greatest threat to life and limb is not a quake setting off an avalanche but the unique climatic conditions the volcano creates, which make lightning strikes comparatively common.

Japan has several ski areas on active volcanos, including Mount Aso, which claims to have been the first place in the world to have built a cable car on an active volcano back in 1958. Mount Kusatsu-Shirane, where a man died in an avalanche set off by an eruption in January 2018, also saw gondola windows smashed by flying rocks. There's also New Zealand's Mount Ruapehu (see page 242), which last erupted in 2007. Snowboarders also have the opportunity to go 'volcano boarding' on a slope of volcanic pumice on Cerro Negro, an active volcano near Leon in Nicaragua.

Of the many inactive volcanoes you can ski, Mauna Kea in Hawaii is perhaps the most rewarding experience.

Despite Hawaii's sun and surf reputation, with its peak being 4,207 metres (13,802 feet) above sea level, there's usually a good snow covering on Mauna Kea in winter, although there are no lifts, just observatories, at the top. Be careful not to continue skiing off the snow, as the land beneath is sacred to the native Hawaiians. Mauna Kea is actually the tallest mountain in the world, measuring around 10,000 metres (32,808 feet), about a mile higher than Mount Everest. It's just that most of Mauna Kea sits beneath the Pacific.

EL CÓNDOR, CERRO CASTOR

ARGENTINA

Tierra del Fuego is familiar to most as the famously stormy sea around the southern tip of South America, but it shares its name with a province of Argentina, home to the city of Ushuaia, where most of Cerro Castor's skiers and boarders are based. It's from here that cruise ships and more serious tourists and adventurers head off to Antarctica. Ushuaia (which is around 3,000 kilometres/2,000 miles south of capital Buenos Aires) was once the world's most southerly city. But in 2019, neighbour and rival Chile upgraded the small hamlet of Puerto Williams to city status, so it took the title, nominally at least.

Cerro Castor is not only the world's most southerly ski resort (subject to debate), beating Ben Lomond and Mount Mawson on Tasmania by a few degrees, but it's also one of the newest, opening in 1999. That relative youth is reflected in its lifts – more than half of the eight are modern quad chairs, unusually impressive for a South American ski area of its stature. And particularly so since, as the story goes, the first lifts shipped from Europe were washed overboard in containers, and more needed to be ordered.

The slopes are south-facing and funnel down to the base, so a number are candidates for 'most southerly', but El Cóndor is arguably the best, accessed by the Del Bosque or Del Rio then Las Piedras quads. You can get off at mid-station of the upper lift to jump in near the start of the run, but most stay on to the top for the most magnificent views out over the Beagle Channel and across the Chilean border before descending another black run,

Chimango, then turning skier's right a short way down to ski El Cóndor from the top.

Essentially, this is a magnificent, high-speed, black-rated slope that swoops gracefully down the mountainside like its famous feathered namesake. The upper third is on the open mountain, an area of large snow bowls with some rocky outcrops and exciting chutes that a guide can lead you to. The high-speed cruise then reaches the treeline and continues over a thigh-burning 2 kilometres (1.25 miles) to the base of the mountain where you can hop back onto one of the quads and do it all again.

Cerro Castor usually has one of the most reliable ski seasons in South America, although it is subject to different climatic factors than the continent's most famous ski areas thousands of kilometres north in the Andes. The resort boasts a few metres (6+ feet) of solid snow rather than the 'snorkel deep' dry powder found in the Andes, which is becoming less reliable each winter, alas.

Arguments continue over whether Cerro Castor is the world's most southerly ski area. Before it was created, Ushuaia already had two small ski areas. One of these, Wolfgang Wallner, claimed to be the most southerly ski area in South America. The other, Glacier Martial, is still there and a little further south than Cerro Castor but not really operating as a ski area as such. It does have an aged double chairlift, already second-hand when installed in 1983. But when there's enough snow there is still an unmaintained, fairly easy run with more amazing views out to the Beagle Channel. Technically Glacier Martial is therefore another candidate for 'most southerly lift-served run in the world' but only if you don't require a reliable lift operating, a good chance of snow cover or a groomed surface to qualify.

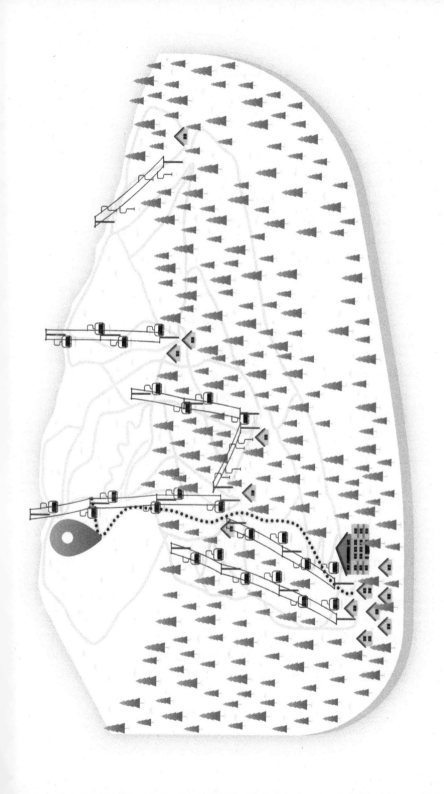

What about skiing a little further south still in Antarctica? Well, there is rather a lot of snow there and its highest peak, Mount Vinson (4,892 metres/16,050 feet), has been conquered by several intrepid skiers in their quest to ski the highest mountains on all seven continents.

Kit DesLauriers, the first woman to ski from the summit of Mount Everest, was also the first person to achieve this feat in 2006. The late Davo Karničar also finished skiing the seven summits a few weeks later in 2006 and is credited with being first, having made complete descents of all seven when DesLauriers did not ski full descents on Everest and Denali . There have been other extreme skiers who have made some remarkable descents of large sloping icebergs off the coast of Antarctica, but most people who ski there for leisure are the super-rich who can afford to hire ice-breaking superyachts like the 77-metre (253-feet) long *La Datcha*, which has its own helipad and can thus cruise off the coast and fly heliskiers in. More affordable (but still quite pricey) options are available from companies such as Ski Antarctica, which uses an expedition yacht to reach the shore and has clocked up more than 140 different Antarctic summits, including over 50 first ascents, during more than two decades.

But there are, or at least have been, ski lifts on Antarctica. In his excellent 1992 book, the *South America Ski Guide*, author Chris Lizza tells of portable ski tows at scientific camps run by New Zealanders and Americans on the White Continent for leisure use in their downtime. However, there have been more recent reports that use of the American lift is being discouraged because scientific expeditions can't risk a ski injury when the nearest medical help is months away.

Chris also reports on a fixed lift, a second-hand T Bar, being installed by the Chilean Ski Federation, with help from the country's air force, for the community of Villa Las Estrellas, the largest civilian settlement on the continent (year-round population 80) and located towards the northerly tip of Antarctica. There was some fanfare around the opening of the lift, Chris reports, with the famous American skier Billy Kidd (one of the first two Americans to win Winter Olympic medals in an Alpine ski race, taking silver in the 1964 Innsbruck Games) flying in especially. The lift accessed a 60-metre (197-feet) vertical on a slope called Cerro Franciscano.

A final note on Cerro Castor. The name translates to 'Beaver Mountain' and is named after 50 beavers which were introduced into the wild here in the 1940s with the aim of kick-starting a fur trade. Alas, with no predators they instead grew to a current population estimated at 100,000 and are blamed for destroying some 16 million hectares (39.5 million acres) of forest with their dams.

EL AGUILA, SIERRA NEVADA

SPAIN

Sierra Nevada is Europe's most southerly major resort and also one of the most joyous. It lies right on the Mediterranean coast and, as you drive up from the old town of Granada through almond and olive groves, it's hard to imagine you're going to find snow, let alone ski runs above. Granada is a university city, home to 80,000 students, many of whom hit the slopes whenever they can, so there's plenty of energy and laughter about.

Sierra Nevada has Spain's highest slopes, climbing to nearly 3,300 metres (10,827 feet), hundreds of kilometres from the next nearest ski area. The first storm clouds arriving from the Atlantic will hit, many of them choosing to dump abundant snow on its slopes as they are forced to rise. In good years, despite the Mediterranean sunshine, the resort can stay open until May and boasts Europe's deepest snowpack, sometimes reaching 6 metres (20 feet) by the spring. In bad years, Sierra Nevada operates one of Europe's largest snowmaking systems.

From the mountain base at Pradollano (one of Europe's highest at 2,100 metres/6,890 feet), there's a choice of gondola lifts up to the mid-mountain base at Borreguiles, which provides access to half a dozen more lifts to the upper slopes as well as numerous slopes back down. Continuing on up to the top of the ski area via the Veleta II chair and then the Zayas T bar, you reach the highest point of the lifts, just below the Veleta Peak (3,398 metres/ 11,148 feet). Veleta is Spain's third highest peak, with the highest Mulhacén (3,479 metres/11,414 feet), actually the

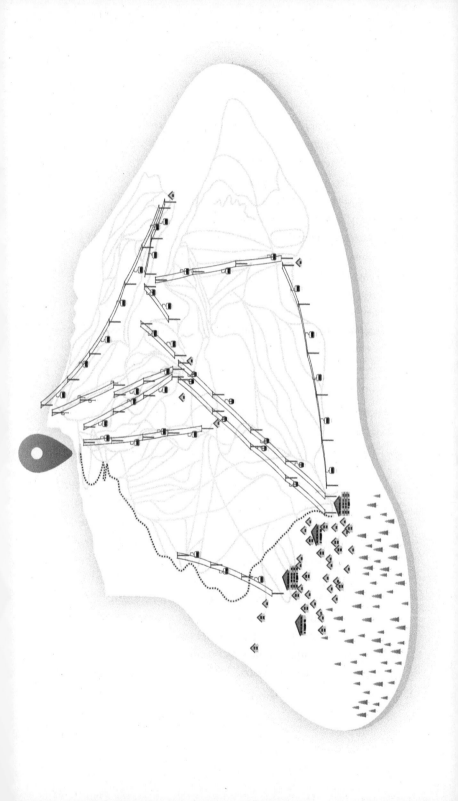

FACT FILE

IN SHORT Europe's most southerly major ski area, and Spain's highest, has views across to North Africa and a wonderful Mediterranean ambience.

DIFFICULTY OF RUN Moderate

VERTICAL OF RUN 1,198 metres (3,930 feet)

LENGTH OF RUN 6.1 kilometres (3.8 miles)

SKI AREA ALTITUDE RANGE 2,100–3,298 metres (6,890–10,820 feet)

RESORT AREA DIMENSIONS 110 kilometres (68 miles)

RUNS 133

LIFTS 21

WEB sierranevada.es

GETTING THERE Rail to Granada, 40 kilometres (25 miles); or Air to Granada, 70 kilometres (43 miles)

highest peak in western Europe outside of the Alps, just next door to the south-east.

This is a key part of the whole ski area, providing access to the resort's longest run, various itinerary (ungroomed) black descents and the Descenso Hombres downhill race-course from the 1996 Alpine World Ski Championships. This is the best spot for looking south, out across the Med, where you may see ships at sea and, if it's a clear day, the coast of Morocco and North Africa's Rif Mountains beyond.

The temptation for good skiers is to turn right off the top of the T Bar and descend to the challenging terrain in the Laguna Valley. The runs here are graded red and black, with several marked off-piste descents too, overshadowed by the craggy Tajos de la Virgen and Cartuja peak. Off-piste ski touring expeditions led by local mountain guides tend to set off into the wider backcountry from here too. It's very different to the rest of the ski area as the runs and indeed the views don't carry on to the resort at the base.

Turn left off the Zayas T Bar, though, and you are on the resort's longest run, El Aguila (The Eagle), which swoops for 6.1 kilometres (3.8 miles) all the way along the boundary line of the resort back down to base. Although officially graded red, much of this can be tackled by a low-level intermediate, and it is essentially a wonderful, fast cruise that starts far above the resort, letting you feel like you're in a world of your own as you whizz down the slopes with empty terrain beyond the Valle de San Juan to your right.

Sierra Nevada's long season means it is still open well into springtime when the daylight hours get longer and the sun melts the snow at most northern hemisphere ski areas. So-called 'pond skimming' competitions are a common end to the season at hundreds of resorts, with skiers and boarders, sometimes in fancy dress, skiing down a short slope and attempting to cross a pool of icy meltwater, to the general amusement of onlookers.

Given Sierra Nevada's big student customer base, it's no surprise that they go one better and stage an annual day of skiing and boarding in swimwear. Normally the last day of the season, and with lift passes heavily discounted for those who arrive for Bañador (swimsuit) Day in swim gear, the day attracts well over 1,000 people. In an even more bizarre twist, Sierra Nevada now goes head-to-head each spring with two Russian ski areas to beat the Guinness World Record for the most people skiing or boarding simultaneously in swimwear. Its competitors are the Siberian ski resort of Sheregesh, along with the 2014 Sochi Winter Olympic venue Rosa Khutor, which calls its own annual swimsuit ski the BoogelWoogel alpine festival. At the time of writing, the number needed to win the record is around 2,000.

If you've got your swimwear on to ski at Sierra Nevada, don't waste the opportunity for a little pre- or post-ski swimming in the Med. The beaches of the Costa Tropical (Motril, Almuñécar and La Herradura) are just under an hour away.

SARENNE, ALPE D'HUEZ

FRANCE

There's a long-running debate among skiers: 'Should the world's longest black run be graded black at all?' It's a great talking point, and the discussion has helped the run become one of Europe's best known and earned it a place on the bucket list of many skiers and boarders.

Sarenne, promoted as 'the world's longest black run', is about 16 kilometres (10 miles) long and drops about 2,000 vertical metres (6,562 feet) with an average pitch of about 12.5 per cent. That sounds more like a blue run than a black. Then when you ski it, apart from a few steep pitches (which aren't really 'black' steep either), you'll think, 'well that wasn't very black, was it?'

Pressed on the matter, the marketing department at Alpe d'Huez patiently explain (for the thousandth time) that the grading isn't so much about the steepness of the run, but about the fact that it departs from the main ski area for most of its length, beginning in high mountain glaciated terrain, so the black grading is really to warn off inexperienced skiers. Sarenne is not like a normal run with branches off and restaurants to stop at every few hundred metres; once you're committed, you have to stick with it for a long, long way.

Sarenne is so enjoyable you won't care what grading it's been given. On a good day, with fresh snow, blue sky and not too many other skiers, it can be one of the best runs of your life. It begins from the highest lift-served point above Alpe d'Huez, accessed by the Pic Blanc cable car up to 3,330m (10,925 feet). The terrain here is so snowsure it offered summer skiing not so many years ago. In good weather, the 360-degree view from the top includes the neighbouring Les 2 Alpes ski resort as well as Pic Bayle, Meije and Aiguilles d'Arves peaks, and even Mont Blanc. In fact, it's claimed that you can see a fifth of France from this peak, but this too is open to debate.

In the immediate vicinity, you'll see the enticing Sarenne slope itself dropping away in front of you. There are many wonderful things about this run, but the best thing is how long you can ski without needing to get on a lift. That 12.5 per cent average gradient is just perfect for a fabulous cruise down the mountainside, on and on, at whatever pace you choose.

Eventually the slope swings around to skier's left and enters woodland in the Gorges de Sarenne, where it becomes a near-horizontal path and you have a choice of chairlifts to take you back out to the main ski area.

Sarenne can get busy at peak times, but it rarely gets overly crowded and most are good skiers and boarders. It's best to head up there when the lifts open so that you're one of the first down. There are other runs departing from there too, almost all black, with several (including Cassini, Château Noir and Cristaux) merging into Sarenne further down. The run to be wary of, unless you are a true expert skier, is Le Tunnel, which takes you through a tunnel (the clue is in the name) to the top of a seriously steep slope, usually mogul-filled.

Debates like the one over Sarenne's grading occur in après-ski bars around the world every night of the season. It highlights the fact that there is no standard measure as to what makes an easy, intermediate and difficult slope. There's not even an international agreement on which colours to use. In most French- and Italian-speaking resorts,

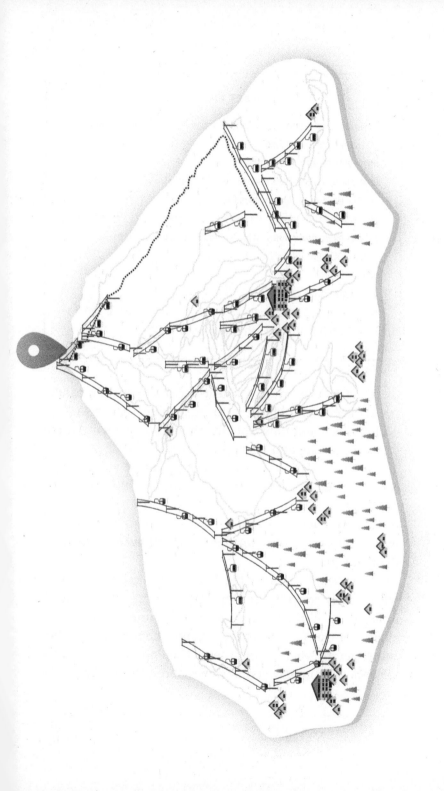

there's a 'very easy' green level, while German-speaking
resorts begin with blue. Confusingly, blue is the next level
up in France and Italy. Luckily, there is agreement on red
for intermediate and black for difficult.

In North America, runs have a symbol as well as a
colour. Easy runs are green circles. Intermediate runs are
not red but blue squares, and the most difficult trails are
black diamonds. Individual resorts sometimes come up
with impressive variations like double or even triple black
diamond runs.

Marketing is another big factor in run grading. Resorts
with mostly steep terrain know they'll lose a large chunk
of business if they don't appeal to families and novice
skiers, so runs that would be intermediate at another
resort get an 'easy' rating there. The opposite is true at a
ski area with mostly gentle slopes and little vertical rise –

there, even slightly steeper slopes can get a black grading. Varying weather and slope conditions are also a factor. A run can be made easy and beautifully smooth by fresh snow one day, and made difficult by sheet ice or carved into huge moguls the next.

At times health and safety legislation has created a tendency to regrade formerly black runs – genuinely steep slopes in some Alpine resorts – as 'off-piste itineraries'. That's partly because it's fashionable to call them 'freeride', but there's also a lower level of legal liability for the resort if something happens off the groomed slopes and colour-coded trails.

As with so many things in skiing, each run is a unique experience.

THE REBLOCHON RUN, LA CLUSAZ

FRANCE

Cheese is a big factor in many people's ski holidays. Of course, it's the key ingredient in many favourite Alpine dishes – fondue, raclette, tartiflette – but a lot of us don't realise the symbiotic relationship between cheese farmers and the Alpine ski business. Many of our favourite cheeses originate in the mountains. Herds of cows graze the ski slopes from spring until autumn, nature's natural pre-season slope preparation. Local farmers are busy with cheese production in the warmer months and then provide accommodation, along with those 'locally sourced organic ingredients', for skiers, and some even go on to work as ski instructors or mountain patrol in the winter.

Cheese lovers can choose their ski destination based on their favourite cheese (although oddly that's not yet an option in ski holiday search engines). For Gruyère, Gstaad in Switzerland is located close to Gruyères itself; or for raclette, picturesque Val D'Anniviers in the Valais canton is the closest ski area to Turtmann, where the best raclette cheese comes from. Beaufortain, a key ingredient in fondue Savoyarde, is available in the French resort of Arêches-Beaufort, where there is a cheese cooperative in the centre of the village. Italy's Trentino region has created a special Dolomites Cheese Route taking in several ski areas, and you can even find 'artisan vegan cheese' produced from organic tree nuts infused with spices, herbs and salts at the Glowfood Creamery in Banff, Canada.

In the modern era of cutting carbon emissions, several resorts use dairy industry waste to generate green power.

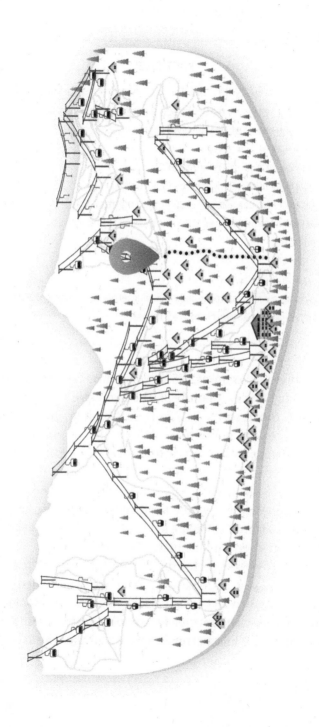

In Killington, Vermont, USA, 'cow power' generated from local dairy farms' manure is the exclusive energy source running the resort's K-1 Express Gondola. In the Swiss Engadin region, home to St. Moritz and several other ski resorts, Europe's highest-altitude dairy, the Lataria Engiadinaisa, sends the whey left over from cheese production to generate electricity: 4,000 tons of waste product used to be shipped to the valley for disposal each year, but now generates around 280,000 kWh of electricity a year at a local green energy plant instead. Pretty clever.

The Aravis ski region of France takes its cheesemaking particularly seriously. In 2021, they unveiled a ski run dedicated to the local cheese culture. The Reblochon Run is actually the former Envers blue piste, a gentle trail running for 2.5 kilometres (1.5 miles) all the way along the edge of the valley, for a total vertical descent of 250 metres (820 feet).

The slope has long been a favourite of old and young skiers alike, providing picture-postcard views, with the village below to your right as you descend past old, traditional chalets from the Étale sector, the Beauregard Forest to skier's left. It's part of the area the local Abondance cows graze in the summer.

There are information boards, games and artworks celebrating the region's 800-year history of farming along the route, which also explain the positive impact farming has on the local environment. You can find details on flora and fauna, get the chance to ring different types of cow bells, and even enjoy a little treasure hunt.

La Clusaz is one of the longest established ski villages in the French Alps. It's part of the Aravis region centred on the picturesque lakeside town of Annecy. The slopes above La Clusaz make up the larger part of a 200-kilometre (124-mile) regional lift pass that is shared with several neighbouring villages, including Le Grand-Bornand.

Both villages have a proud wintersports heritage, supplying many of France's best ski racers, not just in downhill sports but also cross country and biathlon, in which athletes shoot targets in addition to skiing cross-country. Biathlon requires a delicate balancing act of skiing fast enough to win, but also reserving enough energy to hold the rifle straight, as missed targets mean time penalties.

But they're equally proud of their cheese farming, with more than 100 farms in operation covering some 5,000 hectares (12,350 acres) of grazing land (some of it winter ski slopes) once the snow melts, and as many cows as people (over 2,000 of each).

Reblochon was one of the first cheeses in the country to receive the Appellation d'Origine Contrôlée (AOC) certification that means the real product can only be made in a certain location. For champagne that's the Champagne region; for the soft, delicate-tasting Reblochon cheese, it has to come from the eastern slopes of the Haute-Savoie (or one small adjacent valley in neighbouring Savoie), but nearly two-thirds of it is produced in the Aravis Massif.

VALLÉE BLANCHE, CHAMONIX

FRANCE

The world's longest lift-accessed ski run has the same problem that the former world's highest ski run had: climate change. Chamonix in France is a very different proposition in most respects to the now closed Chacaltaya in Bolivia. The Vallée Blanche is an incredible off-piste descent of approximately 20 kilometres (12.4 miles) through phenomenal glaciated terrain. To claim the title of world's longest lift-accessed ski run, it features around 2,800 metres (9,186 feet) of vertical, if you're lucky enough to have good snow all the way down to Chamonix.

The world's former highest ski lift and run were at Chacaltaya in Bolivia, 5,400 metres (17,717 feet) up in the Andes. The primitive lift, originally constructed from an old car engine, set lots of other records too. It was the continent's first, built in 1939, as well as its most northerly. It was also the ski area closest to the equator (which ultimately spelt its doom) and the only one in the southern hemisphere to operate during the northern hemisphere's winter. The old lift, a fast-moving metal cable you had to grab on to, was jokingly called the most difficult on the planet to ride, in part because for many it is hard to do much at all in the thin air at those altitudes.

Chacaltaya's ski run was a very different affair to the Vallée Blanche. At 200 metres (656 feet) it was about 100th of its length, but like the famous French descent, it was built on a glacier. In the latter half of the twentieth century, it was noted that the glacier was disappearing, and in the 1990s they began measuring the decline, calculating that at the current rate of melt it might all be gone by 2015. Actually, it was gone a decade earlier. A tragedy for skiers but more of a problem for about 100 million people living below who rely on glacial meltwater for agriculture, drinking water and to power hydro-electric plants.

Unless you ski it year after year, you won't notice the melting of the Géant, Tacul and Mer de Glace glaciers, the latter the largest in France. They lie under the snow as you descend the Vallée Blanche, a run that's on the bucket list of most skiers and boarders and is tackled by about 50,000 each season.

The Vallée Blanche begins with a two-stage cable car from downtown Chamonix to the remarkable Aiguille du Midi (3,842 metres/12,605 feet) mountain station. The 20-minute ascent of 2,700 vertical metres (8,858 feet) is one of the tallest possible on the planet by lift. The second section of the cable car is also the longest single span cable way there is: 3,000 metres (9,842 feet) without pylons.

Before you even get on the lift you should have hired your guide, strapped on your avalanche transceiver and packed your probe and shovel because you will be skiing over a glacier with hidden crevasses which sadly still take lives all too often. The Arête, for many the most feared part of the Vallée Blanche, is a 150-metre (490-feet) long downhill ridge walk to the start of the run, where you'll need to carry your skis or board. The mountain slopes away precipitously on either side and your guide may recommend crampons and/or roping your group together for security against a slip.

Once nerves ease, you strap on skis or board and follow your guide through the vast glacial landscape of blue ice and magnificent mountain peaks, with little sign of human existence (other than your fellow skiers) for most

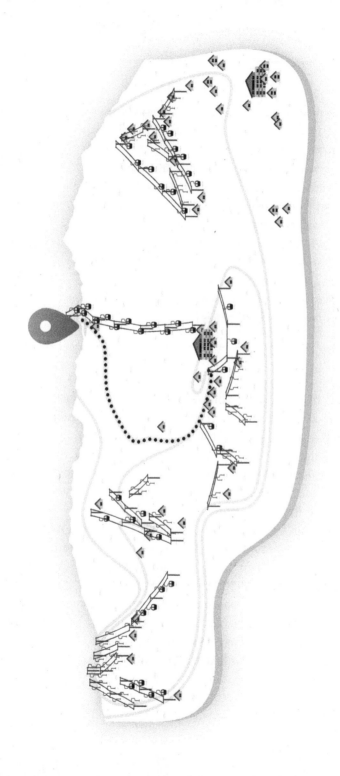

FACT FILE

IN SHORT The world's longest lift-accessed ski run is also one of the planet's clearest markers of climate change.

DIFFICULTY OF RUN Difficult

VERTICAL OF RUN 2,807 metres (9,209 feet)

LENGTH OF RUN 20 kilometres (12.5 miles)

SKI AREA ALTITUDE RANGE 1,035–3,842 metres (3,396–12,605 feet)

RESORT AREA DIMENSIONS 150 kilometres (93 miles)

RUNS 77

LIFTS 68

WEB chamonix.com

GETTING THERE Rail to Chamonix, station at resort; or Air to Geneva, 88 kilometres (55 miles)

of the way down. At the height of winter, in a good year, your guide may be able to lead you over snow (although with a break for a 100-metre (330-feet) near-vertical descent at the end of the glacier) all the way back down to Chamonix. For the vast majority, their run ends below the historic Montenvers hotel and railway station, after 1,600 metres (5,250 feet) of vertical descent, where they face the infamous staircase out.

In the 1980s, a short gondola was built down to the level of the ice. It was soon noted that the gap between the base station of the gondola and the ice was growing, and in the early 1990s three steps were built down to the ice. A decade later, there were 118 steps for your tired legs to climb off the glacier, in your ski boots, carrying your skis. By 2010, it was a thigh-destroying 320 steps, and by the 2020s we've reached an incredible 550 steps. For many that staircase climb out at the end of the Vallée Blanche run is now its greatest challenge.

Montenvers is an important place itself in the history of Alpine tourism. In 1741, two British travellers, William Windham and Richard Pococke, travelled there and returned with amazing stories of the spectacular glaciers. This started summer travel to the mountains, initially with transport provided by mules, and the first hotel was created in 1840. By the late nineteenth century, an army of 200 mules was reported to be working on the route, but the train line was inaugurated in 1909 and they were put out to grass.

In 2021, a €54m project was announced for a new gondola to the current level of glacial ice to be built about 700 metres further up the slope, with a 'glaciorium' and climate interpretation centre at the top, due to open in 2023–24. It'll make the world's longest lift-served ski run a little shorter, again a symbol of the ongoing impact of climate change on all things snow sport. At least it means an end to all those steps, for a while.

If Chamonix can ever stop building steps down to the Mer de Glace, we'll know we've beaten climate change.

ORANGE, TIGNES VAL D'ISÈRE

FRANCE

Beyond the usual groups of couples, singles, families and friends found on the mountain, ski holidays can be designed for just about any group. Resorts host women-only weeks, vegetarian or vegan ski holidays and special holiday packages for Christian or Jewish skiers. America has the National Brotherhood of Skiers and lots of groups for older skiers, with names like The Over The Hill Club. Large corporations like Google sometimes book out resorts for a mass ski holiday for their lucky employees, and there are a growing number of annual music festivals in the mountains that bring thousands of clubbers or rockers, some of whom are just there to enjoy life and don't bother to ski at all (how dare they!).

Various gay ski weeks also take place in leading resorts across Europe and North America. Each event mixes snow time with a vibrant après-ski scene, which can get quite wild, and sometimes features skiing or boarding in full drag.

The world's first Gay Ski Week took place in Aspen in 1977 and was an informal affair. Four locals, Jon Busch, David Hoch, Tom Duesterberg and Russell Anderson, got together with gay visitors from various ski clubs (San Diego, Los Angeles and Chicago). Each club took turns hosting parties on different nights to which all were invited, and everything grew from there.

The European Gay Ski Week began in the Austrian resort of Sölden in 2007, and is now staged at different resorts each winter where it attracts over 1,000 people.

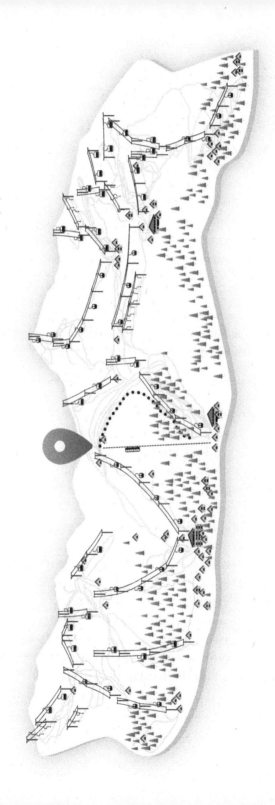

```
┌─────────────────────────────────────────────────────┐
│                     FACT FILE                         │
│                                                       │
│  IN SHORT  One of the world's great ski areas is     │
│       proud of its welcome to all nations, religions  │
│       and those of all sexual orientations too.       │
│  DIFFICULTY OF RUN  Moderate                          │
│  VERTICAL OF RUN  1,009 metres (3,310 feet)           │
│  LENGTH OF RUN  4 kilometres (2.5 miles)              │
│  SKI AREA ALTITUDE RANGE  1,500–3,456 metres          │
│       (4,921–11,339 feet)                             │
│  RESORT AREA DIMENSIONS  300 kilometres (187 miles)   │
│  RUNS  153                                            │
│  LIFTS  82                                            │
│  WEB  europeansnowpride.com / valdisere.com /         │
│       tignes.net                                      │
│  GETTING THERE  Rail to Bourg-St Maurice, 30          │
│       kilometres (19 miles); or Air to Chambery,      │
│       142 kilometres (89 miles)                       │
└─────────────────────────────────────────────────────┘
```

European Snow Pride, one of the several claiming to be 'the biggest gay ski week in Europe', has taken place across the vast Tignes-Val d'Isère ski region each year (other than during the pandemic, of course) since 2008. A highlight is always the parading of a vast rainbow flag down the slopes. The original rainbow flag, devised by artist Gilbert Baker in 1978, had eight coloured stripes, but the most common versions today have six: in red, orange, yellow, green, blue and violet. Red, green and blue runs, and often yellow 'itinerary routes', are common on ski maps across Europe, but an orange category is not, so it's lucky that the region has a red run called Orange which is regarded as arguably the best intermediate run at the resort. It's located just on the Val d'Isère side of the ski region, dropping down from the Rocher de Bellevarde (2,827 metres/9,275 feet) around the open slopes of La Spatule to end at La Daille, just over 1,000 vertical metres (3,280 feet) below.

Orange is a glorious descent, largely taking place on the open mountainside, initially staying above the Marmottes chairlift (which brings skiers and boarders over from Tignes) before dropping below it and plunging away to the right, following the natural mountainside round and down towards the treeline above La Daille, staying to skier's left of the gondola lift that ascends back up from the valley floor.

It's tempting to ski the whole run at speed if conditions are good and the slope not too crowded, but it also takes you close to the legendary La Folie Douce après-ski cabaret bar and restaurant, so perhaps on the next lap around it's only right to pay homage to this legendary establishment – the original of a growing chain across the Alps.

Gay skiers and boarders have spoken passionately about how the mountains offer an added sense of freedom to their lives, and how enjoying this with their peers makes the experience better still. 'For many, skiing and snowboarding epitomises feelings of freedom and self-expression. For the LGBTQIA+ community, these are sentiments not taken for granted and there is a huge demand for spaces that are guaranteed to be welcoming, inclusive and where LGBTQIA+ people can relax, be themselves and just have fun,' Kevin Millins, Event Director of The European Gay Ski Week, told news site Qweerist in February 2019.

Aspen's Gay Ski Week has also played a part in the ongoing civil, legal and human rights battle for the gay community in the USA. Over almost half a century, organisers are proud to have welcomed the LGBTQIA+ community into the ski world, and to have influenced both district and supreme court judgements towards the progress of equality and a more inclusive, tolerant world.

Over the decades, gay ski weeks have come under fire themselves for a perceived focus on muscles and drag at the expense of the wider LGBTQIA+ community. The Arosa Gay Ski Week in Switzerland, established in 2005 and one of Europe's longest-running, has made a particular effort in recent years to offer more for the lesbian community.

Today there are gay ski weeks staged in most countries, the largest in resorts like Mammoth, Telluride and Whistler, where they are often a cornerstone of the season's listing. 'Snowmosexuality' has never been more accepted or celebrated.

FRANCO BERTHOD, LA THUILE

ITALY

Ski resorts have a long tradition of April Fool jokes, as 1 April ties in with the final weeks of the season for the majority of ski areas.

In 1974, a local prankster in Alaska, having spent three years shifting old tyres into an extinct volcano above his town, set light to them to fake an eruption. It was impressive enough for a coastguard helicopter to be sent out to investigate. The pilot read the words 'April Fool!' spray-painted on the snow in 15-metre (50-feet) high letters as he flew over the cone.

More recent April fools have been targeted at social media with the hope of going viral. The ski holiday company Crystal announced ski resorts were putting double yellow lines on the sides of ski slopes to prevent people from taking a rest on the way down. Another, Iglu, which sells both winter sports and cruise ship holidays, put the two together with an impressive picture of a snowy ski slope as a new attraction on an ocean liner. Ski manufacturer Salomon released skis designed for two people to use simultaneously, a kind of skiers' tandem. Then the famous indoor snow centre Ski Dubai focused on the current interest in space travel by announcing it was opening an indoor ski centre on Mars (most people spotted that one wasn't very likely quite quickly). There have been many, many more.

Ski areas in France, where the joke is famously known as the '*poisson d'avril*', are particularly keen on the concept, and on 1 April 2021 the resort of La Rosière was splashed across newspaper and web pages with an image of a smiling team of resort staff unearthing a massive tusk from the snow. It was proof at last, they said, that Hannibal had passed through their ski area as he marched his elephants over the Alps into Italy.

Like all the best April Fools this contained an element of truth. The fact is, in 218 BC the 28-year-old Hannibal and his army, accompanied by 37 African battle elephants, marched from southern Spain to Italy. Rather than taking the expected route along the Mediterranean coast, they surprised the Roman army by crossing the Alps instead. It was the start of the Second Punic War between the then mighty North African empire of Carthage and fast-growing Rome for control of the region – 500,000 people died and Hannibal, despite his elephants, lost.

What no one knows for sure is where exactly Hannibal crossed the Alps. There were no reports until nearly a century after the event, but scholars have narrowed it down to several likely routes. Scientists, analysing local organic matter, have found DNA evidence that a large herd of animals passed along one of these routes about 2,200 years ago – they're just not sure if it was Hannibal.

The good news for skiers is that several of the candidate crossing routes are now lined with ski lifts and pistes (the lifts might have made it easier for Hannibal and his army, if not the poor elephants). One possible crossing route comes at Col du Clapier, located at the end of the ski area of Val Cenis; a second is located between the French resort of Montgenèvre and Italy's Claviere. The latter is the gateway to the huge Via Lattea or 'Milky Way' ski area, which expands over 400 kilometres (248 miles) of linked slopes, mostly on the Italian side, home to famous resorts like Sauze d'Oulx and Sestriere, and host to the 2006 Turin Winter Olympics.

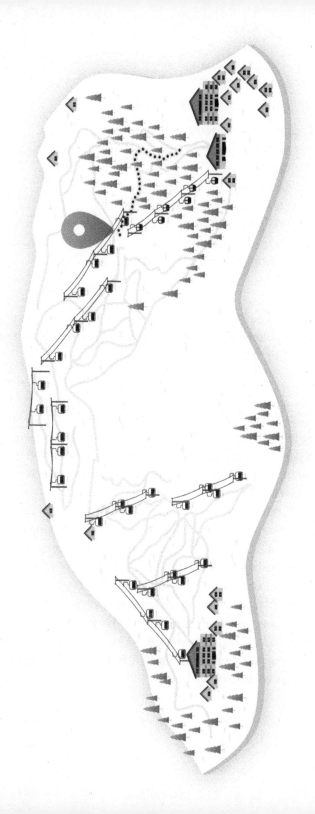

FACT FILE

IN SHORT Follow the route of Hannibal and his elephants (probably) from France down one of Italy's most notorious World Cup runs.

DIFFICULTY OF RUN Difficult–Expert

VERTICAL OF RUN 707 metres (2,320 feet)

LENGTH OF RUN 2.3 kilometres (1.5 miles)

SKI AREA ALTITUDE RANGE 1,650–2,800 metres (5,413–9,186 feet)

RESORT AREA DIMENSIONS 3,000 hectares (7,413 acres)

RUNS 82

LIFTS 38

WEB lathuile.it / larosiere.ski

GETTING THERE Rail to Aosta, 48 kilometres (30 miles); or Air to Turin, 156 kilometres (97 miles)

There is probably a one-in-three chance that skiers in these two regions are skiing the same slopes that Hannibal's elephants crossed. However, if you want to pick a run to really celebrate it, there are few better than the women's World Cup downhill piste into La Thuile at Europe's other cross-border French–Italian ski region, the Espace San Bernardo. This links La Rosière to La Thuile over a vast, sometimes windy plateau. It is further north than Hannibal's most likely route, with plenty of space for an army and a herd of elephants, but it's easy to imagine the vast army charging down into Italy as the plains opened up below them.

The slope is named after Franco Berthod, a local up-and-coming ski racing star of the 1960s, who debuted in the World Cup at a very young age but sadly had his career cut short by injury.

It is one of the most challenging Italian ski slopes, with a gradient hitting 76 per cent at its steepest part (31 per cent on average over its full length). The run has good snow cover thanks to its location perpetually in shade through midwinter, often making it harder, faster and icier, and thus more challenging still. Signs at the top of the run warn that it is suitable 'for expert skiers only'.

If you base yourself in La Rosière, skiing across to La Thuile is a great day trip. Set off early and you can buy true Italian pasta or pizza over the border by lunchtime. Once you've skied down into La Thuile, you have, almost certainly, followed the route into Italy that Hannibal took. If anyone doubts you, simply tell them of that tusk discovered in La Rosière.

KANDAHAR, CRANS-MONTANA

SWITZERLAND

Crans-Montana sits in a fabulous position on a sunny terrace above the Rhone Valley. A vast swath of the Alps, including most of the famous peaks, is visible from virtually every part of the resort, which was once two villages that have grown together to become one of the world's top ski destinations.

The slopes here are unusual for a northern hemisphere ski resort in that they are largely south-facing, which means that along with the views, skiers and boarders enjoy plenty of sunshine. Sun and snow don't always mix, of course, but the slopes here climb to the permanently ice- and snow-covered Plaine Morte glacier at nearly 3,000 metres (9,843 feet), so that's not a problem.

Run 19, the Kandahar, which descends from the top of the glacier, takes everything in. If you carry on down the mountain to slightly mellower terrain you can ski for a glorious 12 kilometres (7.5 miles), descending nearly 1,500 vertical metres (4,921 feet).

Crans-Montana is very important in the history of Alpine skiing, being one of the world's original ski areas. The latter decades of the nineteenth century and the first of the twentieth century were the formative decades of Alpine skiing, which, unlike its predecessors, rapidly became 'downhill only' for most. The concept was immortalised in the name of Wengen's famous Downhill Only Ski Club, established in 1925 and still going strong today (see Lauberhorn run, page 99).

After the first Brits enjoyed what's popularly regarded as the first winter sports holiday in history in 1864–85 in St. Moritz (see Olympia run, page 114), and Norwegian Sondre Norheim invented the Telemark method of skiing downhill a year or two later, in the 1870s, the first skis were imported to the Alps and local carpenters began creating their own versions.

The next big leap occurred in 1893 when author Sir Arthur Conan Doyle rolled into Swiss resort Davos, which had built a reputation as a health spa. Fellow writer Robert Louis Stevenson had been in town a decade before, reportedly suffering from writer's block, and completed *Treasure Island* there. Conan Doyle decided to try skiing, wrote about it for a popular London magazine, and it became all the rage (see Olympia run again).

In 1902, mountain-holidays pioneer Henry Lunn began organising religious/health retreats incorporating winter sports. Advances in ski design and technique thanks to the efforts of Austrians Mathias Zdarsky in Lilienfeld and Hannes Schneider in the Arlberg lay the final foundations for modern Alpine skiing, with boots fixed to skis at the heel, and two ski sticks rather than one Venetian-gondola-style pole as was used in the early decades.

Crans-Montana enters the story on 7 January 1911, when Henry organised the first downhill ski race in the world there. Lunn had been searching for a location where you could ski on a relatively constant pitch, without too many turns, to avoid falling.

Although a local business had been producing skis for nearly two decades in nearby Glarus, this was, of course, an era long before ski lifts, so the racers set off a day before the race, hiking for six hours up to the hut at Wildstrubel

(2,791 metres/9,157 feet). The race began at 10 the next morning and involved two small uphill sections, the first via Weisshorn-Lücke (2,852 metres/9,357 feet) onto the Plaine Morte glacier (which descended much further in those days). Unlike races today, there was no marked route, you were just required to pass through these three points. Other than that, flags marked the start and end of the course, and the winner, Cecil Hopkinson, completed the first (mostly) downhill race in history in 61 minutes.

Hopkinson was the first to be awarded the Art Deco-style Roberts of Kandahar Challenge Cup donated by Field Marshal Earl Roberts of Kandahar, who had been knighted by Queen Victoria in 1882 for liberating a British garrison under siege in Kandahar province, Afghanistan.

The Field Marshal was a man of huge importance in Victorian Britain at the height of the empire. Following his death a few years later in 1914, aged 82, of pneumonia caught while visiting troops in France at the start of World War I, he became one of only two non-royals in the twentieth century to be given the honour of lying in state in Westminster Hall, the other being Winston Churchill.

He was not, however, a skier, but he gave Lunn permission to name the first ski racing cup after him, on condition that the race concerned was staged in Montana each year, where Roberts had enjoyed a holiday. Lunn, however, moved it to Mürren the following year, perhaps as he had bought a hotel there and had nearly 500 beds to fill.

The Kandahar name has been attached to ski races ever since, lending itself to a famous ski racing club established by Henry's son Arnold, and to World Cup racecourses including the one at Garmisch Partenkirchen, and to Crans-Montana's run 19 where it all began.

Getting to the top of run 19 from Crans-Montana today is a far speedier affair than it was in 1911, taking about 20 minutes. The world of snow and ice at the summit with 360 degree views is very special. Officially graded black, thanks to the high Alpine terrain, the gradient feels more red–blue as you ski down. High above the treeline, this is a glorious cruise for mile after mile.

When you reach the bottom, make sure to pay homage to those intrepid racers of 1911 at the memorial stone erected in the resort on the event's centenary.

THE LAUBERHORN, WENGEN

SWITZERLAND

The Lauberhorn is one of the world's most famous ski races, the first of a series of classics staged in January each year. It has been running for more than 90 years, but unlike the Hahnenkamm at Kitzbühel which usually takes place the weekend after, the Lauberhorn course isn't terribly challenging. Unless you're skiing it at 160 kmh (100 mph) that is. At a nice leisurely pace, it's an absolute pleasure.

The Lauberhorn (2,472 metres/8,110 feet) from which both the race and run take their name, is a mountain in the huge, historic and truly stunning Jungfrau ski region of the Bernese Alps. It's located between the famous resorts of Wengen and Grindelwald with the awesome Eiger, Mönch and Jungfrau mountains towering above.

The course is the planet's longest World Cup race-course at 4.48 kilometres (2.75 miles), about a kilometre longer than the average, and has seen the fastest ever racing speeds recorded on the fastest part of the race-course, Haneggschuss. French racer Johan Clarey reached 161.9 kmh (100.6 mph) in 2013, and the world's best ski racers complete the run in about 145 seconds. The contest is watched by 30,000 fans and millions more on TV around the world.

But if you're not racing for your nation and a place in the history books, as well as the lion's share of over 120,000 Swiss Francs in prize money, the descent has a pleasant average gradient of 14.2 degrees and the scenery around you is breathtaking. There are several excellent mountain huts serving first-rate Swiss refreshments en route, so what's the hurry?

The Lauberhorn racetrack is closed to recreational skiers until after the mid-January race weekend, but after that anyone can ski it. There are several options, one very old and one very new, via which to reach the start of the run. The original route involves travelling on the Jungfrau mountain railway to Kleine Scheidegg, from where you hop on the Lauberhorn chairlift. This railway line opened in 1892 and for decades was one of the few effective ways of getting up a mountain without needing to hike. The Downhill Only Ski Club was formed in Wengen in 1925, enshrining that then rare asset in its name.

The other option is to make use of an exceptionally modern lift, the V-Cableway, which opened nearly 130 years later in December 2020. This is a much faster means of accessing the Eigergletscher railway station, the next stop above Kleine Scheidegg en route to the Jungfraujoch (3,454 metres/11,332 feet), Europe's highest railway station. From here you can quickly ski down to jump on the same Lauberhorn chairlift or get on the Wixi chair, which takes you to the top of the run.

The racers regularly quickly hit 137 kmh (85 mph) on the way down, but you can take it easy and won't need to get airborne at the Russisprung (Russi jump). It's named after Swiss Olympic champion Bernhard Russi. A global figure in ski racing over the past six decades, Russi is also mentioned in the chapters on St. Moritz (page 114) and China (page 215), and could have been mentioned in several others.

For racers, things change rapidly at the Hundschopf (dog's head), the most famous jump on the course, which

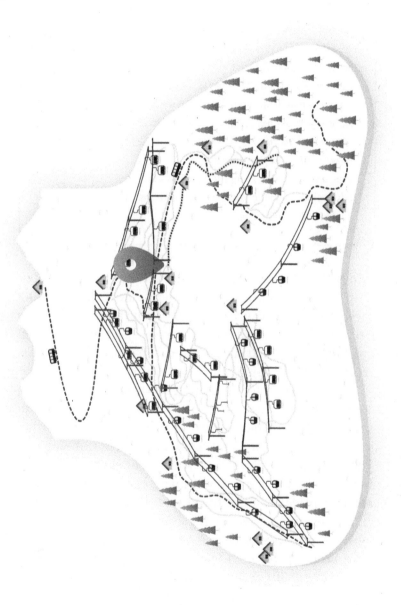

brings the easy cruising to an abrupt end with a sudden drop through a narrow gap between some rocks. At racing speed, this means you are suddenly flying around 20 metres (66 feet) into the air through a narrow space with rocks on one side, safety netting on the other, described by some racers as 'like dropping into an elevator shaft'.

The run becomes relatively gentle again but the Alpweg trail is very narrow, like a single carriageway, with several sharp turns that racers have to negotiate at speeds that would send cars or motorbikes on tarmac spinning off. The piste passes through a small tunnel known as the Wasserstation (water station) under the railway line, and racers consider it lucky to ski under as a train goes over. After the treeline comes the Haneggschuss, the section where the highest speeds recorded in World Cup racing have been set, before a few final tight turns and a small jump into the finish line and the cheering crowds.

The Lauberhorn competition was originally conceived in the 1920s. Local boy Ernst Gertsch, who was born on the first day of the new century on 1 January 1900, played a key role and is credited as 'the Father of the Lauberhorn'. Earlier incarnations of the race existed for several years until it was first run in its present form in 1930. It is, therefore, one of the longest-running ski races in the world. Along with the downhill, the weekend also features slalom and super-combined competitions, the latter including a slalom race and a shortened downhill.

The race continued throughout World War II, although with largely Swiss competitors and some years missed, generally due to bad weather. In 1991, the race was cancelled due to the tragic death of young Austrian skier Gernot Reinstadler in a training accident, and again in 2021 at short notice due to a coronavirus outbreak among the race organising team.

A link to the race on Wengen's website claims Gertsch created the race 'to prove the Swiss could beat the British, which they promptly did'. This is mostly true, though actually a Brit, Bill Bracken, won the first-ever Lauberhorn combined race (awarded for the best finish in both a slalom and a downhill race), but no other Brit has won there since. Unfortunately for the Swiss, a glance at the winners over the past 60 years shows Austrian dominance. Famous names to have won the downhill three or more times include Austrians Toni Sailer, Karl Schranz and Franz Klammer, and Switzerland's Beat Feuz.

The great American racer Bode Miller won twice in 2007 and 2008, famously crashing and crossing the finishing line spinning on his side to take his first victory there. He calls the Lauberhorn 'the essence of skiing'.

PISTE 10, MÜRREN

SWITZERLAND

There are a remarkable number of connections between the world of James Bond and winter sports. Ski resorts have not been slow to pick up on this, and besides simply visiting the filming locations, you can stay in a James Bond-themed hotel room, visit a mountain top interactive 007 exhibition, watch a film in a 007-inspired cinema, eat 'James Bond Spaghetti and Meatballs' in a mountain restaurant, ski down a specially named 007 piste and even visit a 007-themed public toilet in ski resorts across Europe.

But one resort owes more to the Bond franchise than any other. The classic Swiss resort of Mürren (see Klammer's Run, page 152, for a little more on its importance in the early years) had fallen on hard times by the mid-1960s. A plan emerged to revive its fortunes by building a cable car to the Schilthorn (2,970 metres/9,744 feet) with the world's first revolving mountain restaurant on top. However, the project ran out of money and the restaurant was incomplete when the Bond team working on *On Her Majesty's Secret Service* (1969) stepped in with an offer to finance the restaurant's completion in return for using it as a major location for the film. More than five decades later Mürren remains grateful.

Mürren's black run number 10, which descends from the Piz Gloria revolving restaurant (it was named after the fictional mountain lair in Fleming's book) on the Schilthorn summit, is something very special indeed. Unlike most ski area peaks, there's no alternative but this black

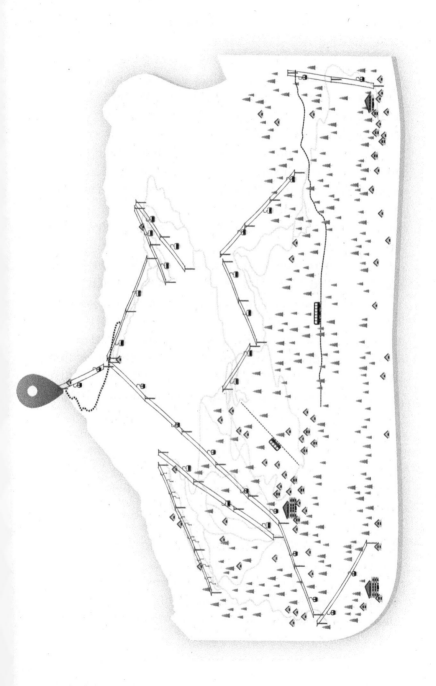

graded steep option down – other than going back in the cable car, that is.

You will want to take in the stunning views from Piz Gloria of the spectacular Jungfrau and Eiger peaks before you descend, and perhaps visit the Bond World exhibition on the lower floor or venture out onto the more recent 007 Walk of Fame, added in 2015.

You feel like you're on the top of the world as you set off down the run. It starts narrow, with a sign advising you of gradients reaching 75 per cent, and large nets protecting you from the precipitous drop, before you pass under the arriving cable car, initially following the ridge before dropping below to the left.

Those incredible views remain along the same slopes that were used in the film more than 50 years ago. Below the lower cable car mid-station at Birg, you'll pass the start point of the famous Inferno run. The Inferno is the world's longest downhill ski race, which attracts 1,850 amateur competitors each winter, racing to the valley floor at Lauterbrunnen over a 14.9-kilometre (9.25-mile) course, as it has done since 1928 (although there were fewer racers back then).

Bond author Ian Fleming lived for more than a year in the famous Austrian resort of Kitzbühel in the 1920s. You can still book into his room in the resort's Tennerhof Hotel nearly a century later and attend the annual 'Fireball' celebration of Bond there each winter. In his penultimate Bond tale, *You Only Live Twice* (1964), Fleming reveals that Bond's father, Andrew, was from the ski area of Glencoe in Scotland, his mother, Monique, Swiss.

Skiing reappears often in the film franchise. Roger Moore's James Bond famously skied off a cliff to unfurl a Union Jack parachute at the start of *The Spy Who Loved Me*

IN SHORT James Bond is making his presence felt in more and
more ski areas as the franchise ages, but none has the
heritage and scenery of Mürren.

DIFFICULTY OF RUN Expert

VERTICAL OF RUN 330 metres (1,083 feet)

LENGTH OF RUN 1.6 kilometres (1 mile)

SKI AREA ALTITUDE RANGE 790–2,970 metres (2,592–9,744 feet)

RESORT AREA DIMENSIONS 51 kilometres (Jungfrau region:
211 kilometres / 132 miles)

LIFTS 16 (Jungfrau region: 63)

WEB muerren.swiss / schilthorn.ch / jungfrauregion.swiss

GETTING THERE Rail to Mürren, station at resort; or Air to Zurich,
112 kilometres (70 miles)

(1977), and down the Olympic ski jump and bobsleigh run
at Italy's Cortina d'Ampezzo in *For Your Eyes Only* (1981).
Moore himself was a long-time resident of Swiss resort
Crans-Montana, which now features a large mural of him
as Bond, and there's a private Bond-themed Sir Roger
Moore cinema in the five-star Guarda Golf Hotel.

Moore was still playing Bond in 1985's *A View To A Kill*,
which is credited as being the first mainstream movie to
feature snowboarding. Pioneer Tom Sims was the stunt
double riding the board which, it was pretended, Bond had
repurposed off the front of a snowmobile.

The next Bond actor, Timothy Dalton, did not spend
too much time on skis, although he did slide across a
border through the Iron Curtain in a cello case in *The Living
Daylights* (1987). It was Pierce Brosnan who got Bond back

on the snow a decade later. His second Bond outing, *Tomorrow Never Dies* (1997), begins with a huge battle in a remote Russian military mountain airport, apparently in Afghanistan but actually filmed at the French Pyrenees resort of Peyragudes. The ski centre unveiled a piste number 007 to celebrate the twentieth anniversary of filming in 2017.

Two years later, *The World Is Not Enough* (1999) depicted Brosnan jumping from a helicopter onto a virgin snow slope, purportedly in Azerbaijan, but filmed in Chamonix. The crew obtained special permission to use helicopters for filming in the mountains, not usually permitted in France. A major avalanche hit the Chamonix Valley as filming was taking place and the crew immediately stopped and used their helicopters in the rescue effort instead.

Daniel Craig's *Spectre* (2015) was shot in the Austrian Tirol, particularly the resort of Sölden. Craig didn't ski so much as crash-land a large plane and use it as a giant sledge to knock out armoured Land Rovers like a bowling ball hitting skittles. The film takes in Sölden's uber-stylish Ice-Q glass mountain restaurant, 3,048 metres (10,000 feet) up, and we see Q riding a gondola and staying at the Hotel Das Central. Of course, all can be visited, along with the 007 Elements mountain top interactive Bond exhibition created after the film's release.

THE WITCH'S RUN, BELALP

SWITZERLAND

As you are whisked up from the valley floor in comfortable gondolas with their heated leather seats and in-cabin Wi-Fi, it's easy to forget that a little over a century ago these mountains were viewed very differently.

The poor farmers (some of their descendants are now millionaire hoteliers) looked to the heights not just in fear of a harsh winter or an avalanche, but all manner of supernatural dangers too. Locals who were lost after falling into an unseen glacial crevasse were believed to have been snatched by demons. One Swiss resort, Les Diablerets, today famed for its fabulous glacier ski area, was named simply as a warning: it translates from the French as 'the home of devils'.

For another Swiss resort, Belalp (a name with a much more promising translation: 'beautiful Alp'), the problem wasn't devils but witches. Well, one in particular (although apparently they did burn quite a few). Legend has it that a witch disguised as a local woman, at Hegorn in the Natischerberg Mountain, decided to marry a pious man, but then couldn't help herself and fell in love with a sorcerer too. To carry out their affair in secret, the witch and sorcerer turned themselves into ravens whenever they planned a surreptitious rendezvous. One day, the witch, busy boiling soup in a cauldron 3,000 metres up at the top of the local Aletsch glacier, realised she was out of garlic. With no grocery delivery app available, she changed herself into a raven and flew down to her garden in the valley for a fresh clove. As she reached the garden she saw her husband up a cherry tree picking the ripe fruit. Then, in the kind of catastrophic set of events you only find in Swiss legends, the raven-formed witch accidentally deposited some bird droppings at the very moment her husband decided to look to the heavens to pray to the Lord. Unsurprisingly, disaster ensued, the bird-poo-blinded husband fell from the tree and died instantly.

It was an open and shut case as far as the village elders were concerned. They were apparently not suspicious of the poo bombs in the husband's eyes, his broken bones nor the whole woman-raven thing, but a cauldron high up in the mountains was a clear sign of witchcraft. The verdict: she was to be burned at the stake.

In our civilised and enlightened times, that witch's fate is widely seen as something of a mistrial. Any decent lawyer today would have got her off on involuntary mariticide, not least because apparently when you're an enchanted raven you've no idea when bird droppings will happen. There's also some suspicion due to the fact that village elders kept the assets of families where a witch was discovered, which may have influenced their decision-making slightly. Belalp today is therefore doing all it can to make amends and belatedly clear the witch's reputation.

A superb ski run, the Witch's Piste begins at the top of the slopes 3,118 metres (10,230 feet) up at Hohstock, the spot where the cauldron was boiling away, possibly, and ends at Kühmatte, still 2,047 metres (6,715 feet) above sea level. Over its 633 vertical metres (2,076 feet) of descent, the run eases from a quite steep and challenging upper section, to much more mellow terrain as you reach the treeline and enter the mountain forest (alas, there are no cherry trees to be seen).

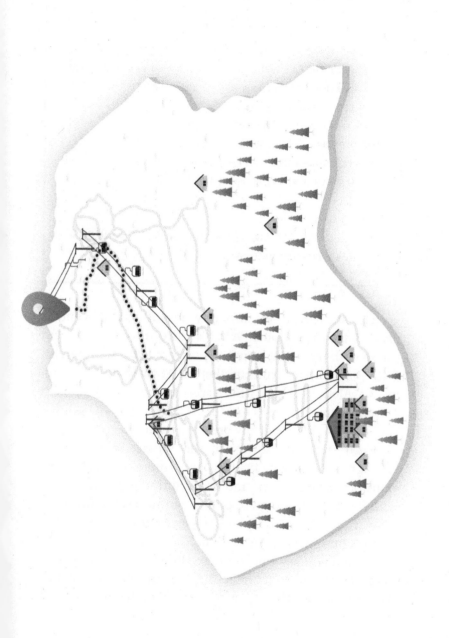

FACT FILE

IN SHORT There are many myths and legends in the Alps, and at Belalp you can fly the route once flown by a witch disguised as a crow, dressed as a witch, if you'd like?

DIFFICULTY OF RUN Moderate

VERTICAL OF RUN 1,796 metres (5,892 feet)

LENGTH OF RUN 12 kilometres (7.5 miles)

SKI AREA ALTITUDE RANGE 1,322–3,118 metres (4,337–10,230 feet)

RESORT AREA DIMENSIONS 60 kilometres (37 miles)

LIFTS 11

WEB belalp.ch

GETTING THERE Rail to Brig, 5 kilometres (3 miles); or Air to Geneva, 224 kilometres (140 miles)

The difference in difficulty means the descent is divided into the Upper Witch's Piste (Häx Oben – run number 3), rated black, and the red-graded Lower Witch's Piste (Häx Unten – run number 4). At these altitudes, up by the Aletsch glacier (the largest in the Alps still with 11 billion tons of ice and a UNESCO World Heritage site), the snow quality is usually great all season.

Turn right at the top of the Witch's Run and ski through a 150-metre (492-feet) long tunnel just below the Hohstock peak to access another beautiful piste, number 1, with perfect terrain for freeriding enthusiasts. It descends away from the rest of the slopes before rejoining the Witch's Run in its lower section.

In mid-January the resort celebrates a week of witch-themed festivities, culminating in the 'Hexenabfahrt' (Witches' Race). Described by the Valais regional tourist board as 'one of the biggest and most unusual downhill races in Switzerland', it has been running since the early 1980s and now attracts up to 1,500 people, many dressed in witch costume, wearing scary masks and carrying brooms, to race the 12 kilometres (7.5 miles).

The racecourse follows the route of the witch's piste, then continues down to the village of Blatten in the valley, 1,800 vertical metres (5,905 feet) below. The finish line is believed to be the exact spot where the pious husband fell from the cherry tree.

The length of the race and the vertical descent means you do have to be fairly fit to tackle it, and you'll see serious racers in skintights suits whizzing down ahead of those in fancy dress. But there are plenty of prizes for things like best costume as well as fastest witch. In recent years there have even been spin-offs, such as a culinary version of the race.

Don't worry, the Swiss stopped burning witches in the late eighteenth century. That said, if you hear someone shouting 'D'Häx isch los', it may be time to make your excuses: it translates as 'the witch is out/loose'. But more likely you'll just fall under the spell of this spectacular region.

OLYMPIA, ST. MORITZ

SWITZERLAND

The tale goes that in the summer of 1864, a humble innkeeper in St. Moritz bet a group of English summer holidaymakers that if they visited in winter they'd find plenty of sunshine and fresh air, much nicer than grey, smoggy London. If they didn't agree at the end of their stay, their holiday, including travel, would be free.

Those first winter tourists stayed four months, returned tanned and invigorated and telling anyone who'd listen about their great winter holiday. The innkeeper, Johannes Badrutt, won his bet and began a dynasty that became the legend of St. Moritz. Badrutt built luxurious hotels with all the latest amenities, while St. Moritz itself became one of the world's best-known ski resorts, hosting two Winter Olympics and five Alpine World Championships over the past century – that's more than anywhere else.

But can St. Moritz be considered the first ski resort? The jury is out and much depends on how pedantic you want to be (and skiers love to be pedantic). Winter sports tourism took off quickly in the village. Within three years the first English ice skating club had been established, followed by the first curling club in 1880, and the incredible Cresta Run, an ice run for toboggan racing still handmade each winter, was first created in the winter of 1884–85. But was anyone skiing?

The resort's library contains pictures of Alpine skiers from 1893, including one of the Reverend Camill Hoffmann, the first director of the St. Moritz Tourist Board.

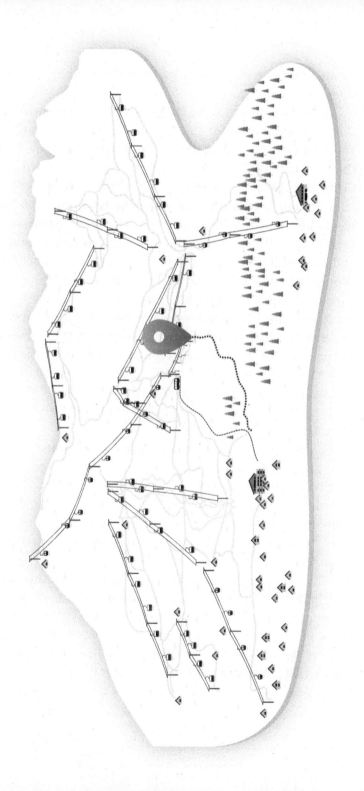

Camill and those in the early snaps may have been the first skiers in the resort.

Another famous resort, Davos, may have had downhill skis, adapted locally for the Alpine slopes, a little earlier. The first Davos winter guests arrived from Germany, and the first pair of Telemark skis from Norway arrived for Christmas 1883, a present to Wilhelm Paulcke – who later became a geologist and avalanche researcher – from his father. Local versions of these skis were made and raced over fairly flat terrain. In 1889, brothers Tobias and Johann Branger began teaching themselves downhill skiing, famously practising at night for fear of being ridiculed by fellow villagers for their crazy idea. They were ski touring by 1890 and their exploits were made famous in 1894 when they led Sherlock Holmes author Arthur Conan Doyle on a route they'd found over the Maienfelder Furka Pass to Arosa and back. His resulting write-up of the adventure is credited as starting the British love of skiing. Back in St. Moritz, the British Ski Club was founded in 1901/02.

St. Moritz hosted the second Winter Olympic Games, in 1928, largely on land surrounding the now huge Kulm Hotel St. Moritz, founded by Johannes Badrutt. Early downhill skiers, as well as tobogganists, also benefited from the construction of one of the first funiculars in 1913, to Chantarella, which was extended with a second stage up to Corviglia.

This latter section contained one of the first funicular lifts built specifically to serve skiers and was a factor in St. Moritz hosting their first Alpine World Ski Championships in 1934, two years before Alpine ski competitions became part of the Winter Olympics at their fourth staging in 1936. When St. Moritz staged the Winter Olympics

a second time in 1948, the resort's Olympia slope became
famous. The route of the original men's downhill on the
slopes of Corviglia down to Chantarella was regarded as
particularly difficult compared to earlier racecourses.

Today, more than seven decades later, the Olympia
piste still largely follows the original route, but because
the ski area has grown so much it is now located more
on the edge of the prepared slopes than it once was. The
upside is that it is in a much less crowded location than
the mountain's other slopes and good skiers will often
get the slope to themselves.

To get to the top of Olympia, take the Corviglia funicular, as skiers have been doing for almost a century. From
here many ski straight on down, take the cable car further
up or head off to the left, but for Olympia, you need to turn

right. It's a thrilling run first over the open mountainside then sweeping right towards the Chantarella, the top of the first stage of the funicular. Old movie reel footage of the 1948 downhill shows what's changed (the run is usually smoother now than it was then) and what hasn't (not much).

The Olympia piste is an Olympic downhill course suitable for most reasonably good skiers, but the resort's current World Cup downhill course is not. Conceived by former World and Olympic Alpine downhill ski racing champion Bernhard Russi, it's a still faster, even more spectacular descent. The run starts from the very top of the cable car at Piz Nair that connects with the top station of the Corviglia funicular. Named Free Fall and constructed over two years before St. Moritz hosted the 2003 World Championships at which it made its debut, the first 150 metres (490 feet) of the course plunge down at 45 degrees (100 per cent), the steepest start of any World Cup racecourse.

The result is that racers hit about 100 kmh (62 mph) within 4 seconds and reach 130 kmh (80 mph) after 130 metres (426 feet). It's not just the racers taken to extremes either; the grooming tractors that keep the slope smooth have to be connected by metal winch cable anchors to stop them sliding off down the mountain. Even TV crews filming the action are tied to the mountainside for safety.

Racers complete the 3-kilometre (1.9-mile) long course in around 100 seconds, spending an average of 10 seconds of that time in the air.

SUPERPANORAMICA, APRICA

ITALY

In midwinter, when there's little or no daylight in Scandinavia and other northerly ski areas, skiing floodlit runs is the norm. There can be other reasons for floodlighting too. In Japan, during the boom years of the 1980s, some ski areas operated 24 hours a day to keep up with demand, which in addition to the lighting often required several lifts to serve a single slope. A similar scenario plays out today in countries like China and South Korea.

Keystone claims the largest night skiing operation in Colorado, and in the US Midwest it's not unusual for night skiing to be offered past midnight, including on New Year's Eve, allowing visitors the chance to ski into the New Year. Cascade Mountain in Wisconsin heroically kept the lifts turning to 4am on 1 January 2000.

Italy's Superpanoramica ski slope was already famous for its fabulous views (hence the name) before its ski resort, Aprica, in the province of Sondrio in the Lombardy region of northern Italy, decided to add floodlighting along its 6-kilometre (3.75-mile) length. This created what is believed to be the longest night skiing slope in Europe.

During the daytime, the run provides magnificent sweeping views out over the village and the valley to the mountains of Valtellina and the entire Rhaetian Alps beyond. At night there are twinkling lights below and, on clear nights, the moon and stars above for a magical experience. Superpanoramica is wide and smooth, carving a zig-zagging path down through the forest and the mountainside of the Corteno area, descending a very satisfying

700 vertical metres (2,297 feet) in total. The slope is popular with everyone from ski school groups through to racers.

The floodlighting of Superpanoramica didn't come cheap. The resort splurged a reported €1m on the project, which included upgrading the chairlift and ensuring high-quality snowmaking along the route. It was completed for the 2020–21 season but eventually opened in December 2021 once skiers took to the slopes again after lockdown.

Aprica's decision to create Europe's longest floodlit ski slope in the 2020s is quite rare. Most of the resorts that have built a reputation for night skiing did so back in the 1970s and 80s when ski areas were expanding in number and size around the world. These days focus is more typically on energy-efficient lightbulbs and switching to green energy; floodlit ski slopes are not the best for a resort's environmental credentials.

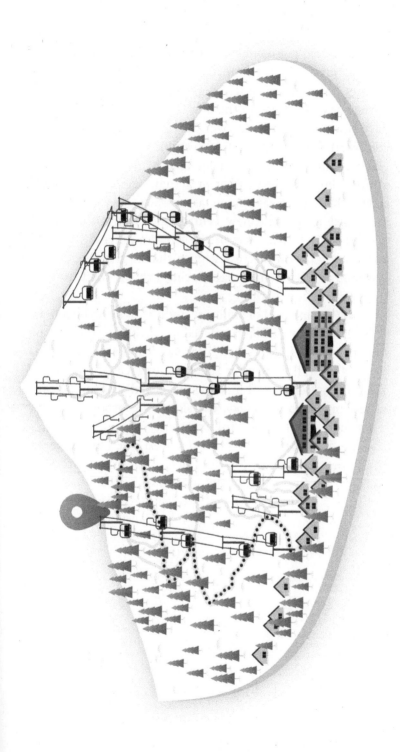

The world's growing number of indoor snow centres are perhaps the least environmentally friendly, being 100 per cent reliant on floodlighting. These first appeared in their modern form in the late 1980s and more than 150 have been built since in over 30 countries and on every continent except Antarctica. Keeping a giant fridge cold and floodlit does require a lot of energy, but a growing number buy in green power or actually generate it themselves through means such as massive solar arrays on their vast roofs. One new centre, Snø, near Oslo, which opened in 2020 with one of the world's longest slopes at 505 metres (1,656 metres), argues that it generates more green electricity than it uses. Perhaps this is the future of snow sports in a warming world?

Another method of skiing at night is to do so by moonlight. Full moon skiing is offered at a growing number of resorts every 29.5 days. La Clusaz (see The Reblochon Run, page 74) is well-known for their sessions. Of course, if the skies are not clear, full moon skiing usually has to be cancelled, but if you're lucky, the slopes are brightly lit and it's a surreal but wonderful experience.

The final option is to pop on a head torch and hike up the slopes yourself, as the most determined ski tourers do to enjoy the first turns of the morning.

THE SMUGGLER'S RUN,
ISCHGL TO SAMNAUN

AUSTRIA/SWITZERLAND

Although some of the world's best-known ski areas were created from nothing specifically to provide ski holidays, most had a former life, often as simple mountain communities. Some grew in status because of a quirk of fate in their location, perhaps providing the only sanctuary on a perilous mountain pass or because the warm, healing waters of a mineral spring bubbled up nearby.

In the case of neighbours Ischgl, in Austria, and Samnaun, in Switzerland, the border location and the different rate of taxation on each side were the crucial factor. The clue is in the name of the ski run that links them: The Smuggler's Run.

Despite its location in the canton of Graubünden, until a century ago, Samnaun could only actually be reached from Austria, as there was no road up to it on the Swiss side of the border. That wasn't a problem, with trading continuing happily between Samnaun and its Austrian neighbour until 1848, when someone far away had the bright idea of introducing customs and import/export tax.

The 'Samnauners' were less than impressed with this new Brexit-like complication to their lives and limit to their freedoms. They mounted a four-decade-long campaign to go back to how things were previously, finally scoring a major success in 1892 with the awarding of duty-free status, the only village in Switzerland to have it.

The first road up to Samnaun on the Swiss side of the border was eventually opened in 1912, and the village

---

started to become popular not just for the scenic drive up, but for the tax-free petrol at the top. These days it is quite surreal as you approach this pretty Alpine village to encounter large motorway-service-style fuel stations.

In the years immediately after the war, life was hard in the Paznaun corner of the Austrian Tyrol where Ischgl is located. Smugglers would carry meat, butter and furs to Samnaun from the Austrian farms in rucksacks weighing up to 50kg, returning with duty-free luxuries like cigarettes, chocolate, coffee and American nylon stockings, as well as hard-to-get basics such as rice and flour. Former smugglers tell of customs officials, who often came from the same communities, not trying very hard to catch them, everyone just doing what they could to make ends meet.

In 1952, things began to change with the construction of Ischgl's first ski lift, part-financed, allegedly, from the smuggling trade. Former smugglers became ski instructors, and today's skiers and boarders can still ski the routes taken by the smugglers, only now with lift assistance and smoothly groomed slopes. The runs, glorious long blue cruisers with a red alternative, descend from the border at Viderjoch (2,740 metres/8,990 feet), passing Alp Trida (2,263 metres/7,425 feet) before converging into run 60 down into Samnaun. Returning on the lifts for the descent back down over the ridge to Ischgl, you have the option of boarding one of the world's few double-decker cable cars, which was installed in 1995 to cope with the mushrooming demand.

Usually, you can ski The Smuggler's Run from the very start of the season in late November, thanks to the altitude. On average about 5,000 people cross the border on the run each day in high season, and the recommendation

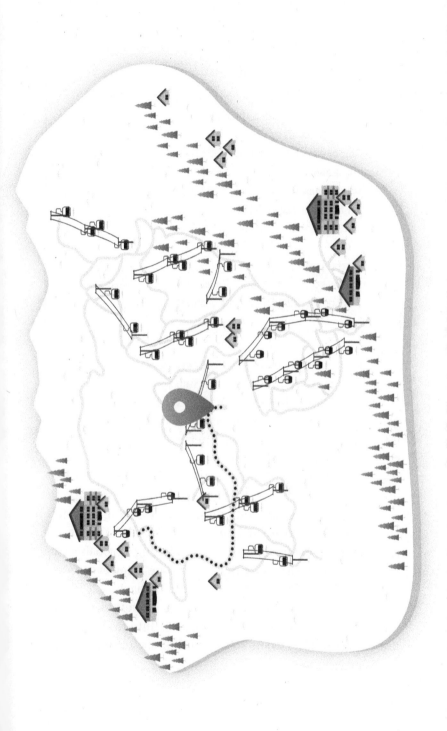

FACT FILE

IN SHORT Follow the route of smugglers across the Austrian–Swiss border and return with your duty-free haul.

DIFFICULTY OF RUN Easy

VERTICAL OF RUN 1,327 metres (4,354 feet)

LENGTH OF RUN 8 kilometres (5 miles)

SKI AREA ALTITUDE RANGE 1,377–2,872 metres (4,518–9,423 feet)

RESORT AREA DIMENSIONS 515 hectares (1,273 acres)

RUNS 239 kilometres (150 miles)

LIFTS 45

WEB ischgl.com

GETTING THERE Rail to Landeck, 29 kilometres (18 miles); or Air to Innsbruck, 100 kilometres (63 miles)

is to start early from Ischgl, especially if you want to do some duty-free shopping on the Swiss side.

These days Ischgl offers a choice of multi-run 'Smugglers' routes' graded easy (bronze 19.8 kilometres/12 miles), intermediate (silver, 24.7 kilometres/15.5 miles) or most challenging (gold, 37.2 kilometres/23 miles). There are prizes to be won and you can track progress on your phone (probably not what real smugglers would recommend).

Like the ski area itself, Samnaun's enticing duty-free shops have gone from strength to strength and there are now around 40 plush retailers, including 'probably the highest tax-free shopping mall in Europe'. However, when you ski back over the border with your backpack full of cigarettes, perfume and alcohol as a modern-day smuggler, it's important to be aware of your duty-free shopping limits if you don't want to fall foul of the customs team.

They are based in probably Europe's highest customs office at 2,756 metres (9,042 feet) altitude – right by the slopes. Spot checks are rare, but goods are confiscated if found.

Another quirk of Samnaun was the annual Santa Claus World Championships that took place at the start of the season for more than 20 years until its final staging in 2021. Teams of four Santas from around the world competed in various *It's A Knockout*-style contests, all in the spirit of Christmas. It was an equally hilarious, bizarre and wonderful competition that made a stay in Samnaun in late November just that bit more surreal.

The early decades of winter sports in the region were a bit stop-start but Ischgl credits the arrival of British skiers in numbers in the late 1970s as the turning point. The past four decades or so have seen the shared ski region, the Silvretta Arena, grow into one of Europe's larger and most snow-sure destinations, open from November to May. It's also one of the best equipped, with a fleet of fast, modern, queue-gobbling lifts rivalling the best in the world.

The hundreds of millions invested in ski infrastructure since the 1980s would no doubt shock the impoverished farmer-smugglers of old, some of the descendants of whom are now very wealthy indeed. One recent particularly dry autumn, when many famous ski areas in the Alps had to delay opening for lack of snow, Ischgl reputedly spent huge sums simply on making snow in order to open as planned. In fact, it claims to be one of only a few ski resorts that has never had to delay its opening.

How times have changed from the days of the smugglers.

BLACK IBEX, KAUNERTAL

AUSTRIA

Skiers love to debate stats and tick ski areas off their lists that boast the largest, highest, longest, snowiest, fastest runs or lifts or mountains. Sometimes these stats are undisputable but often there are provisos that allow for argument. The highest lift-served skiing in the world, for example, is very much open to debate. Most lists include lifts to high places where someone was once photographed with a pair of skis, but does that make the spot a 'ski area'?

The world's steepest ski run is another subject to argue over at length in the après-ski bar. One problem is that there are two different ways of recording gradients: the slope percentage and the number in degrees. The former is the larger and thus more impressive-looking number, but it is harder to compare two slopes when one uses degrees and another percentages. The Austrian resort of Mayrhofen's Harakiri run is publicised as having a 78 per cent gradient for example, but that's just under 38 degrees.

When it comes to slope percentages, 100 per cent is equivalent to a 45-degree angle. Steeper than that and you're at higher than 100 per cent. But are we comparing the average gradient of an entire run or just its steepest part? Often the two are confused. For example, the Free Fall downhill racecourse from Piz Nair above St. Moritz (page 114) begins with a 150-metre (492-feet), 45 degree (100 per cent) drop but then levels out considerably for an overall pitch of around 17.3 degrees (31 per cent).

The next conundrum is the question 'what is a ski slope?' Are we talking any slope with snow on it or a

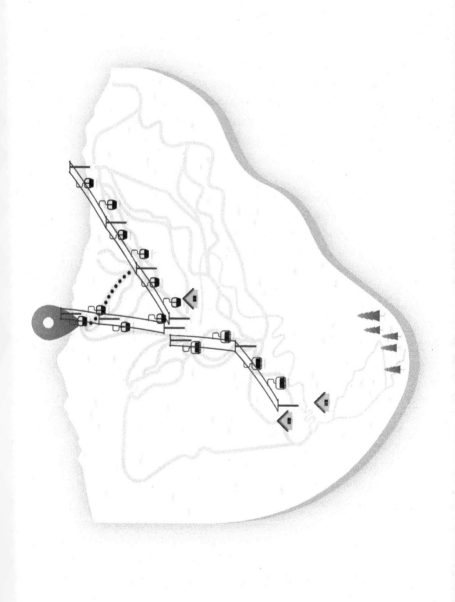

marked slope that can be groomed by a piste-basher? To create the latter, a specific kind of trail-groomer known as a winch-cat is secured by a metal cable to an anchor point at the top of the run and lowers itself down like a large metal spider on a thread. Without that anchor, the winch-cat would just slide off down.

If there are no rules we get into claims that steep chutes or tree-skiing slopes should be included, or very steep slopes outside ski area boundaries, perhaps incorporating a cliff jump or two. We've all seen incredible films of extreme skiers descending what appear to be near vertical 'slopes'.

The past decade has seen a battle fought in Austria over which of its ski areas has the steepest slope. It began when Mayrhofen unveiled Harakiri, which is still thought of as the steepest by many, even though other resorts have

---

unveiled steeper. The latest contestant, Black Ibex, is high up on the Kaunertal glacier in the country's Tirol region. The short, sharp run has an average pitch of 87.85 per cent . . . or 41.3 degrees. There are plenty of famous runs with steeper sections, but none that claim a constant pitch that's steeper. Over Black Ibex's 400-metre (1,312-feet) length you drop 182 vertical metres (597 feet). That's breathtaking for both mathematicians and those skiing or boarding it.

The run begins at the top of the glacier, right on the Italian border, at the top of the impressive Falginjoch funifor lift (3,113 metres/10,213 feet), with magnificent views out over the border into Italy. The descent is a straight adrenaline rush. It's on the open glaciated mountainside high above the treeline and much of the rest of Europe, so it's just you and that very, very steep slope.

Lest you think Kaunertal is all about expert-level terrain, the mountain's glacier runs are mostly blues, with a few reds. It's a ski area that's open up to eight months of the year, from early autumn to late spring, thanks to its glacier. So you can ski steep slopes here when those in most other resorts around the world are closed.

The ease of skiing a steep run anywhere, of course, will rely on the snow cover on the slope. With a hard, icy surface it can be dangerous, easier to fall on and then more difficult to arrest your slide. Soft snow will also slide down a steep run more quickly and easily, scraping the cover bare. For this reason, it's often the steepest runs at a resort that take the longest to build cover, and are the most frequently closed through the season. Many resorts famed for having steep terrain don't open it until late in the season.

Avalanche danger is another major factor. Studies have shown that the vast majority (97 per cent) of 'skier triggered avalanches' have occurred on slopes with a gradient of more than 30 degrees (58 per cent).

4 – 3 – 2 – 1A, HINTERTUX

AUSTRIA

Most skiers and snowboarders spend the summer planning their next trip, then the autumn nervously watching the weather reports hoping for a good pre-season snow dump. There are, though, 30 or 40 ski areas in Europe and North America where the seasons are longer. These are the high-altitude resorts with glaciers beneath their higher runs that can stay open in summer, and indeed spring and autumn too.

The effects of climate change means that there are only about half the number of resorts staying open in the summer than there were back in the 1990s. And the growth of indoor snow centres means there are five times as many places to ski indoors than out these days; by the start of the 2020s there were over 100 operating indoor snow centres in more than 30 countries on six continents, some now larger than the smallest outdoor areas.

At the time of writing, there are still two resorts in the Alps that endeavour to open their ski slopes 365 days a year: Zermatt in Switzerland, home to Europe's highest lift-served runs, and Hintertux in Austria.

It's fascinating watching the snowline falling, climbing, then falling again through the year at Hintertux. This bastion of snow sports in the beautiful Ziller Valley has two main mountain stages: at 2,100 metres (6,890 feet), a 600-metre (1,969-feet) vertical climb from the base; then at 2,660 metres (8,727 feet), from which the final lifts climb to the highest point at 3,250 metres (10,663 feet). This upper third is the year-round section; the middle third stays open about half the year, the bottom winter season only.

This run, actually a succession of pistes, is, almost uniquely therefore, a descent you can start on any day of the year, though you'll reach a different endpoint depending on the season. From late autumn to early spring you can double the length of your descent. Getting to the top involves riding three successive high-speed gondolas, known as Glacier Bus 1, 2 and 3 respectively. These are fast, high-capacity 'funitel' models – a kind of cross between a gondola and a cable car (tram), carrying 24 passengers per cabin and supported on twin cables for added stability on windy days. Wind can be a problem at these altitudes and is the type of weather most likely to close the slopes.

At the top of Glacier Bus 3, you can go inside the glacier, entering an ice cave by climbing down 25-metre (82-feet) ladders onto the ice. There are natural wonders, ice sculptures and the chance to ride an inflatable boat along a narrow tunnel filled with freezing (but somehow not frozen) water. In winter, you can ski all the way to the valley station, some 1,750 vertical metres (5,741 feet) below.

There are around 6,000 ski areas in around 80 countries across the world (nearer 100 if you include those with either indoor snow only like Dubai or Egypt, or those with artificial surface slopes like Brazil and Mexico). The precise number is impossible to know as there are always new ones opening in countries such as China, and small village lifts being taken out of service thanks to old age and climate change on the lower hills of central Europe or eastern North America. The vast majority – 98 per cent of ski areas – are in the northern hemisphere; there are only around 100 in total in Australia, New Zealand, southern Africa and South America.

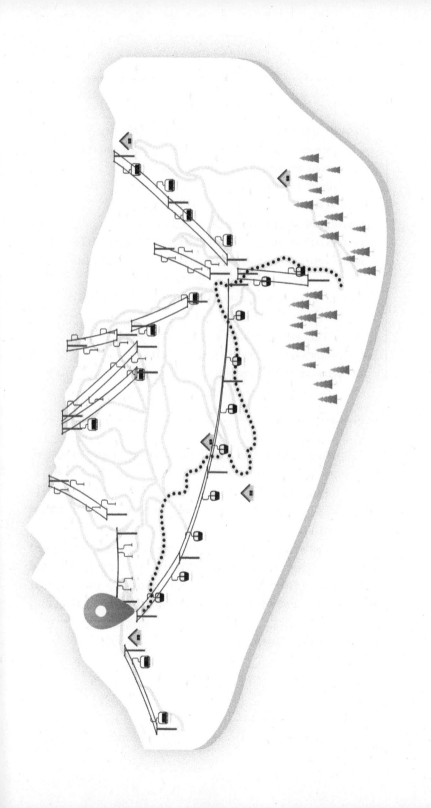

FACT FILE

IN SHORT One of a handful of runs that's open 365 days a year, weather permitting, and one of the world's greatest lift-served descents in the main ski season.

DIFFICULTY OF RUN Moderate

VERTICAL OF RUN 1,750 metres (5,741 feet)

LENGTH OF RUN 12 kilometres (7.5 miles)

SKI AREA ALTITUDE RANGE 1,500–3,250 metres (4,921–10,663 feet)

RESORT AREA DIMENSIONS 235 hectares (581 acres); (185 kilometres/ 115 miles in Glacier World Zillertal 3000 region)

RUNS 61 kilometres (38 miles); (185 kilometres/115 miles in Glacier World Zillertal 3000 region)

LIFTS 21 (57 in Glacier World Zillertal 3000 region)

WEB hintertuxergletscher.at / tux.at / Zillertal.at

GETTING THERE Rail to Mayrhofen, 18 kilometre (11 miles); or Air to Innsbruck, 90 kilometre (56 miles)

Ignoring indoor and artificial surface slopes, most of which operate year-round, there's an annual rhythm of ski areas opening and closing around the world, in the northern hemisphere mostly from mid-November to mid-May, in the southern from mid-June to mid-October.

So there's always a ski area open somewhere, even though in that hinterland between the northern and southern hemisphere seasons from mid-May the number can drop to single figures, sometimes as low as five. But Zermatt and Hintertux are always among them, however low the number goes.

THE HIDDEN VALLEY,
CORTINA D'AMPEZZO/ALTA BADIA

ITALY

Sometimes, there are so many remarkable things about a ski run that it's hard to know which aspect to lead with. And there's no run on earth where this is more true than the exceptional Hidden Valley piste in the Dolomites, a UNESCO World Heritage Site.

That said, the key thing about this run, official name the Armentarola piste, is that it is simply wonderful. Located on the border of two mighty Italian regions, Veneto and South Tyrol, where the language changes from Italian to German (although the local people all speak the traditional language of Ladin anyway), it drops down for 8 kilometres (5 miles) of marvellous skiing as you descend from the ski area of Cortina d'Ampezzo, ending up at the bottom at Sciaré near San Cassiano in Alta Badia, on the edge of the famed Sellaronda circuit.

There are plenty of satisfying 8-kilometre (5-mile) long descents at ski areas around the world, but none like the Hidden Valley. Arriving from Cortina's fabulous ski area, you reach the top of the descent at Lagazuoi (2,835 metres/ 9,301 feet) via a dramatic cable car ascent, climbing against nearly a thousand vertical metres of rock face. These are the highest ski slopes in the region and have the reputation for the light, powdery, deep snow cover you'd expect at these altitudes.

The Hidden Valley run itself, slope number 1 on the map, is graded red and perfectly skiable by anyone with a few weeks of skiing under their belt. It's a groomed slope and of a fairly consistent pitch. Before you set off down, notice the alarming precipice you've just ascended and you might see a network of caves (the entrance is often half-buried in snow). Soldiers were stationed here through the bleak winters of 1915–17, when Italy declared war on the Austro-Hungarian Empire. The caves were carved out by hand, and it's hard to imagine what life must have been like living in them through those years. The area where you're skiing was the scene of conflict.

This was all nearly 50 years before the cable car was installed in 1964 and the Hidden Valley run was officially inaugurated in the mid-1970s. The complete opposite of the depravations of a mountaintop during a wartime winter, you'll also find the enticing Lagazuoi mountain refuge here. Apart from offering scrumptious local food and drink, there are wonderful 360-degree views from the terrace. You have the option to stay the night there too, for fantastic starry skies free of light pollution and the chance to try Italy's highest sauna.

On your descent, you will see no sign of human civilisation, just pine woodland, rock and ice falls, and areas of unique natural beauty, such as at Grande Lagazuoi and Fanes Valley where, on a clear day, the sunshine provides one of nature's great wonders, the pink illumination of the mountains, known as the 'enrosadira'.

Halfway down the slope, as you cross an invisible line to enter Alta Badia, there's another gourmet stop to be made at the Ütia Scotoni mountain hut, run by the Agreiter family for more than 50 years and famed for its grilled specialities cooked on a barbecue in the centre of the restaurant. The hut is also known for its extensive

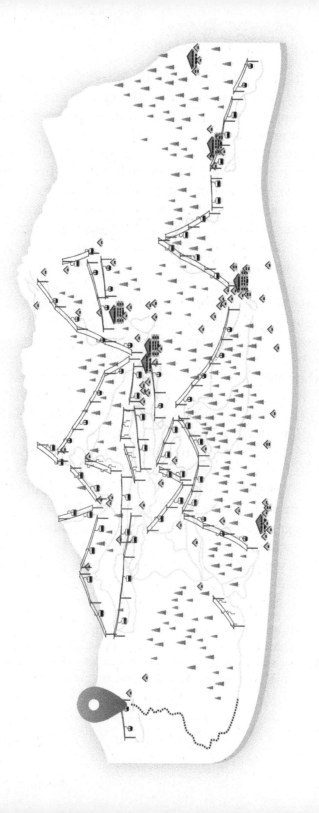

wine list, but before perusing the more than 300 vintages you may wish to sample 'ega', the Ladin name for water which appears here in abundance from Europe's highest water fountain at 2,148 metres (7,047 feet).

Until very recently a bus trip was required to reach the Cinque Torri sector of Cortina's slopes, from which you make your way over to Lagazuoi, but a new gondola connection was completed for winter 2021–22. Aside from the sheer convenience, this adds another claim to fame for the Hidden Valley. It has become a key link in what is now, probably, the longest inter-connecting route of lifts and ski slopes in the world.

At the bottom you'll see there are no lifts back up and indeed no conventional lift from the base. This is a one-way trip. If you wish to return to Cortina you need to take a bus or a taxi, but the temptation is to carry on to the Sellaronda* via a unique horse-powered drag lift. Yes, it really is a pair of horses pulling a rope contraption that you and a dozen other skiers grab hold of to be gently towed, skijoring style, for a kilometre or so. It uses heavy draft Noriker horses native to the Alpine valleys between Italy and Austria, and began as a service to guests of the local Armentarola hotel in Alta Badia after skiers requested a lift from the hotel's sleighs. In the beginning, one horse was enough to pull the skiers, but demand grew and there are now five teams of horses supplied from local farms working in rotation on the route.

---

* The Sellaronda is a circuit of almost 30 kilometres (19 miles) of slopes, which can be skied clockwise or anti-clockwise. Famous ski valleys such as Badia, Fassa and Gardena radiate off it to create one of the world's largest inter-linked lift and run networks.

FACT FILE

IN SHORT One of the world's most beautiful runs is now part of
probably the longest trip you can make on pistes and lifts,
with a little horse-power thrown in.

DIFFICULTY OF RUN Moderate

VERTICAL OF RUN 1,130 metres (3,707 metres)

LENGTH OF RUN 8 kilometres (5 miles)

SKI AREA ALTITUDE RANGE 1,236–3,269 metres (4,055–10,725 feet)

RESORT AREA DIMENSIONS 120 kilometres (75 miles) Cortina;
130 kilometres (81 miles) Alta Badia; 500 kilometres
(313 miles) Sellaronda; (1,200 kilometres/750 miles in
Dolomiti Superski region)

LIFTS 39 Cortina; 53 Alta Badia; 450 in Dolomiti Superski region

WEB altabadia.org / cortina.dolomiti.org / dolomitisuperski.com

GETTING THERE Rail to Calalzo di Cadore, 50 kilometres (31 miles);
or Air to Venice, 140 kilometres (87 miles)

The specialist ski area cartographer Chris Schrahe has measured the greatest distance possible from Cortina to Pozza di Fassa at 36 kilometres (22 miles), skiing and riding lifts continuously. Schrahe says you can actually go further, 40 kilometres (25 miles) to Alpe di Siusi at the far end of Val Gardena, but that involves a 400-metre (1,312-feet) walk between gondola stations in Ortisei.

If you opt to stay on the Cortina side of the mountains, Hidden Valley forms part of an excellent itinerary known as the Super8 Ski Tour, which takes you on more great skiing around the famous Dolomite peaks of Lagazuoi, Tofana di Rozes, Fanis, Averau, 5 Torri and Conturines. On the Alta Badia side, you can take a diversion from the

Sellaronda by bus or taxi to the Lagazuoi cable car before using that remarkable horse-powered lift to get back to the area's regular slopes.

GOLDEN POWDER/GOLDEN RUSH, SPORTGASTEIN

AUSTRIA

Mining and skiing go hand in hand in many locations around the world. 'White gold' – ski parlance for abundant snowfall – can help defunct mining communities enjoy a renaissance thanks to a successful ski resort development. In the US West, property built on land you couldn't give away a century ago can now cost tens of millions of dollars – all thanks to skiing.

Aspen is one of the best examples of this. Before 1880, it was known as Ute City and offered summer hunting grounds for the native Ute peoples. After silver was discovered it was rechristened Aspen and within a decade was supplying a sixth of the US's and a sixteenth of the world's silver. Things fell apart with an economic depression in 1893 and the town stayed largely in the doldrums for the next five decades until the ski area was established.

Many more resorts have origins in coal mining towns, for example powder-paradise Fernie in Canada or La Thuile in Italy's Aosta Valley (page 89). Other ski resorts are found on former iron ore, lead, silver, tin and even salt mining settlements. Essentially, if you could mine it, there's a ski area that once did.

There are also instances of current 'mega-mines' investing in ski lifts as a leisure activity for their workers. Chapa Verde ski area in Chile was originally built for workers at the El Teniente copper mine, the largest underground copper mine in the world with over 3,000 kilometres

(1,865 miles) of tunnels that produces around half a million tons of copper each year.

Across Europe and Asia, municipal authorities struggle with what to do with old spoil heaps from mining works. Many have now been turned into year-round urban ski areas, either with an artificial surface slope laid on top, or a whole giant refrigerated building where snow can be made indoors. What would the miners toiling away in the dark below have made of that?

Austria's Gastein Valley references its gold mining heritage with its ski run names. Your day begins by boarding the Gold Mountain lift (Goldbergbahn), which takes you, over two stages, 1,066 vertical metres (3,497 feet) up to the top of the mountain. Unfortunately, the gondolas' cabins don't have a gold paint job, but you forget all that when looking out over the 400 surrounding Alpine peaks of the Nationalpark Hohe Tauern.

Freeriding on ungroomed slopes is both more pleasurable and more dangerous. The resort has set up a Freeride Info Base, essentially a live digital information board, at the top of the lift with the latest information on conditions, what's open and what's closed, and the all-important avalanche danger level. There's even a facility to double-check your avalanche transceiver is working normally.

The Golden Powder run descends above a famous gold vein for a fabulous 5 kilometres (3 miles) on west-facing slopes. The average gradient, a little under 15 per cent, is not overly challenging and when conditions are good this is just endless floaty powder joy. If you still have bounce in your knees you can get straight onto the second of the golden runs, Golden Rush, which takes you all the way to the base for the full vertical of over 7 kilometres (4.5 miles).

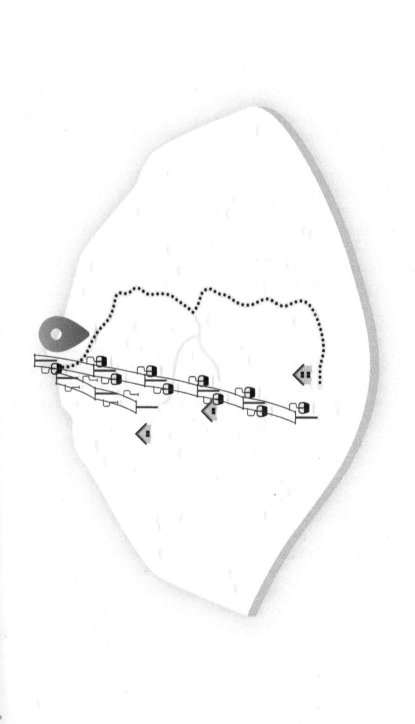

Safety is paramount for the local lift company. As well as requiring skiers and boarders to carry an avalanche transceiver, probe and shovel (and to know how to use them), they maintain an avalanche training centre at the base station in Sportgastein. Skiers and boarders can practise using their transceiver under realistic conditions any time, free of charge and without needing to book ahead.

The Austrians also take breakfast very seriously and there's a weekly opportunity to enjoy it at the top of the Kreuzkogel. You'll notice a curious glass-aluminium dome sat at the summit which was created by architect and designer Gerhard Garstenauer. Within this remarkable structure a very hearty breakfast, including fresh dishes prepared from local regional ingredients, is served.

Sportgastein is part of the wider Gastein area, one of Austria's largest with 200 kilometres (125 miles) of groomed runs. The key resort in the region, Bad Gastein, has 'Bad,' meaning 'bath', in its name for a reason. Its spa waters were popular for centuries, and the late nineteenth century saw kings, queens and emperors visit to take the waters, which Marie Curie, no less, was responsible for declaring contained radon, leading to radon therapy beginning in the town. So after a day floating through powder, there's nothing better than heading to the spa for a soak.

You may also be tempted to try a little gold mining, of course, and gold is still occasionally found here, but it's perhaps best to wait until the snow melts.

GAMSLEITEN 2, OBERTAUERN

AUSTRIA

In the early years, just as the sheer joy of Beatlemania was sweeping the world after decades of post-war austerity, the Fab Four released their second movie, *Help!* (1965). From the base on the slopes of Obertauern, take a ride on the Kirchbühel T bar drag lift and you'll be on the same run that appears in the film. This is one of the village's original lifts and it's little changed since the fortnight in March 1965 when The Beatles wound up in a small cluster of basic hotels to shoot their movie. Now a large statue of the band shows you're in the right place.

Unsurprisingly, the band were not skiers (Paul is apparently the only one who gave it a try). They rode up the slopes on a grooming tractor adapted with a platform on the back. Back then few Brits who weren't from the wealthy classes could hope to go on a ski holiday, but in *Help!* we see John, Paul, George and Ringo sliding down the slope on ski bikes and having endless fun in the snow.

Help! shows The Beatles skiing beautifully, or so it seems. In reality we're watching four young local skiers perform as stunt doubles. For George there was Gerhard Krings, for Paul there was Herbert Lürzer, Ringo's double was Hans Pretscherer and John's was Franz Bogensperger.

Although John, Paul, George and Ringo wouldn't have been up to it, Gerhard, Herbert, Hans and Franz would have had no trouble tackling run G2 on the map: Gamsleiten 2. It is one of Europe's steepest mogul slopes. Unusually, thanks to the abundant snowfall for which Obertauern is famed, it is an ever-changing descent with

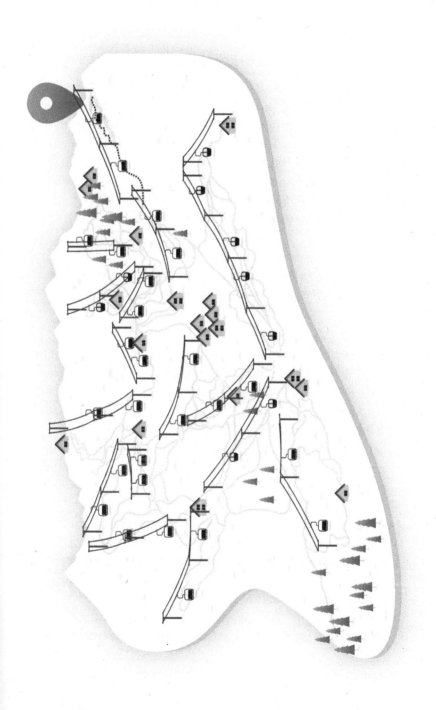

its surface constantly remodelled as it is tackled by skier after skier. Whenever you ski it though, it's always tough, even for the most experienced.

Although Obertauern today is filled with comfortable, fast chairlifts ascending from a resort chock-full of upmarket hotels and restaurants, a rare vintage double chairlift makes the climb to the top of the run, marked 26A on the piste map.

Once you're on Gamsleitenbahn II, there's only the steep way down (besides the shame of riding the chair back down of course). It's a superb descent, with a gradient of 70 per cent, offering magnificent views out over the village and far beyond if you're not too busy focusing on conquering the moguls to look.

The reason why Obertauern was chosen for filming Help! is lost in the mists of time. There's a rumour that it was actually Option B after the first choice wasn't available. Obertauern has a reputation for some of the most reliable snow cover in the Alps. This allows it to open from mid-November through to May each season, when many Austrian resorts close by early April, so the filmmakers knew the snow would be reliable. And going somewhere then little-known internationally was probably a smarter move than arriving in an already popular ski resort where the band would be hounded by fans.

So what became of those stunt doubles, Gerhard, Herbert, Hans and Franz? They had, incidentally, never heard of The Beatles when they arrived in Obertauern and had to rush to Innsbruck to buy a cassette tape of their music. Hans emigrated to the US and sadly Franz is no longer with us, but Gerhard's and Herbert's families continue to run several businesses in the resort (Herbert's family manage the Hotel Edelweiss where The Beatles stayed).

As it was, the locals were treated to what turned out to be The Beatles' only ever gig in Austria, an impromptu affair in the Hotel Marietta staged for a crew member's birthday. You'll find historic pictures of the band in nearly every hotel and restaurant in the resort. However, the best collection of Beatles' pictures is to be found in the bar at Hotel das Seekarhaus (many not published anywhere else in world) thanks to an agreement the film company and record label made with its owner, one Gerhard Krings. There are more in the Lürzer Alm – one of the top après-ski spots – owned by Herbert. Meanwhile, the grand piano that features in the film has made its way up to the Grünwaldkopf cable car's top station. Most years there are also concerts with The Beatles' cover bands, and on anniversary years, bigger festivals too.

KLAMMER'S RUN, BAD KLEINKIRCHHEIM

AUSTRIA

Competition, of one sort or another, has been a driving factor in the evolution of snow sports. Cave painting evidence of early skiing hunters in Altay in the Xinjiang region of China has been dated at 10,000 years old (although some archaeologists are sceptical they're quite that old). Actual skis have been found preserved in peat bogs near Lake Sindor in Russia that are dated to perhaps 6,000 to 8,000 years ago. One is preserved so well that a carved elk head is visible on it. Another primitive ski has been found in a peat bog in Hoting in Sweden that is thought to be somewhere between 4,500 and 6,500 years old.

Things began to change in the early nineteenth century with the first ski-jumping contests reported in Norway in the 1840s. The 1860s saw the earliest reports of downhill skiing, with the Telemark technique developed by Sondre Norheim (then known as Sondre Auverson). He is the first man known to have won a skiing competition, taking the prize at a national competition in 1868. Sondre was already in his mid-forties when he won the competition and set the first ski-jumping world record (19.5 metres/64 feet), beating competitors half his age, thanks to his innovations in ski and binding design.

The focus switched to the Alps, particularly Austria, in the early twentieth century, where Mathias Zdarsky and Hannes Schneider pioneered the Alpine version of skiing that we enjoy today. The first slalom races were staged in the early 1900s, then, on 21 January 1922, everything changed again when British ski holiday (and ski racing)

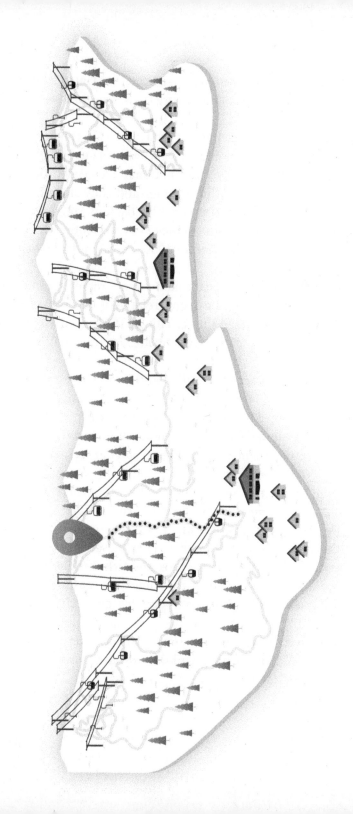

pioneer Arnold Lunn organised the first timed slalom race in Mürren, Switzerland. Before then races had been judged on style, not speed.

Downhill ski racing was not featured in the first Winter Olympics in Chamonix in February 1924, but the world governing body, the International Ski Federation (FIS), was formed during those games and they staged the first Alpine World Ski Championships back in Mürren in 1931. Downhill racing was introduced to the Winter Olympics at Garmisch Partenkirchen in 1936, and then the World Cup circuit began in 1966.

Arguably the greatest name in ski racing, Franz Klammer, appeared on the scene relatively early, making his debut on the World Cup circuit in 1972, aged 19, only six years after the competition had been created. Klammer, a farmer's son from the southern Austrian province of Carinthia, close to the Italian and Slovenian borders, came to ski racing late by modern Alpine standards, starting to compete aged 14. He had a battle to win his place in the national squad, traditionally dominated by racers from the northern provinces of Tyrol and SalzburgerLand.

Franz spent several years 'bubbling under' in World Cup races, not quite taking the win, then everything changed from the Val-d'Isère World Cup downhill of December 1974, with Klammer winning that race and then every downhill after it. That season he won his first crystal globe trophy. He took the title for the next three years and then again in his comeback season of 1982–83 after a five-year lull. Four decades on, that's two more downhill crystal globes than any other male ski racer has achieved (America's Lindsey Vonn has won eight). Klammer's 25 World Cup downhill wins also remains the most ever for a male ski racer.

FACT FILE

IN SHORT A run dedicated to and named after the greatest name in ski racing, who'll even ski it with you if you're lucky.

DIFFICULTY OF RUN Moderate

VERTICAL OF RUN 842 metres (2,762 feet)

LENGTH OF RUN 3.2 kilometres (2 miles)

SKI AREA ALTITUDE RANGE 1,087–2,055 metres (3,566–6,742 feet)

RESORT AREA DIMENSIONS 103 kilometres (64 miles)

RUNS 34

LIFTS 24

WEB badkleinkirchheim.com

GETTING THERE Rail to Villach, 30 kilometres (19 miles); or Air to Klagenfurt, 52 kilometres (32 miles)

But Klammer's legend is not so much about the wins as how he raced, fearlessly and all out. It was this courage, combined with his skill, that made Klammer the skier that everyone dreamed of being. Franz won the biggest and toughest race on the World Cup circuit, Kitzbühel's Hahnenkamm, four times (still a record on the full course). Arguably his most famous victory was at the 1976 Olympics in Innsbruck in front of an Austrian crowd hyped up to fever pitch. Klammer was last of the top seeds to race but won by a third of a second. You can see the race on YouTube or watch the 2021 film, *Chasing the Line*, that builds to that one race.

There are racecourses associated with Klammer victories all over Europe and North America. The one named after him at the resort of Bad Kleinkirchheim, the closest major ski area to his home in Carinthia, was for at least

1,000 years better known for its curative spring waters than its snowy slopes. The spa facilities remain top-notch and a big bonus to a ski holiday here. It's where Klammer used to ski to school from the family farm as a child and won his first race in the inaugural European Cup season of 1971.

The swooping 3.2-kilometre (2-mile) black-graded World Cup run, number 8 on the piste map, with a gradient of up to 80 per cent, was originally known as the 'FIS K70' run, the 70 referring to the year it was created, 1970. Klammer was just 17, but it was not long before the run began to have the nickname 'Franz Klammer'. In 2004 the name was made official, being rechristened the 'Franz Klammer World Cup descent', and the slope was redesigned, with input from Klammer himself.

In contrast to much of the rest of the 103 kilometres (64 miles) of slopes at the area, which is fairly mellow, it's an unrelentingly challenging descent, over 842 vertical metres (2,762 feet), with the large village of Bad Kleinkirch-heim below. The record time for this steep, narrow and fast course is 1:38 minutes, but it's not a good idea to try to beat this.

Klammer has skied his slope at speed many times and these days leads groups of avid fans when the fancy takes him, or the local tourist office asks him to. He has a reputation as a thoroughly nice guy, ensuring no one feels left out, and even offering technique tips to those eager to learn from one of the all-time greats.

WHITE LADY, CAIRNGORM

SCOTLAND

Skiing in Scotland always raises passions. There are five commercial ski centres dotted around the north of the country, and the consensus is that when the snow is good, they are among the best in the world, especially considering the spectacular views to be enjoyed from the slopes.

The difficulty is that the days when the snow is good are increasingly rare. Most agree that this is due to climate change, although some argue that the weather has always been fickle. Scotland's climate can be impacted by strong winds carrying lots of moisture off the Atlantic to the west, and blasts of cold, dry, icy air from the Arctic to the north. The sweet spot is when the two collide and the snow is abundant; then the Arctic air dominates and things stay cold. Too often, though, the Atlantic system dominates, bringing windy and sometimes warm and wet weather which spoils the snow. Environmentalists point to pictures of snowbanks towering over buses taking skiers to the slopes, however we've not seen scenes like that since the 1980s.

But if good snow days are becoming rare in Scotland, it isn't dampening the enthusiasm of local skiers and boarders. Ski touring is booming, with more and more hiking up to ski or splitboard the powder when it's there. Daring to question the greatness of Scottish skiing is considered unpatriotic by many, and the majority of the British ski team over the years honed their skills in the Scottish mountains.

The White Lady is one of Scotland's best-known runs. It's named because the natural snowfield that builds on

Cairngorm each winter resembles the shape of a lady . . . so long as you remember the lady is wearing a wide-brimmed hat, a large trailing skirt and has her arms outstretched. She's facing towards the northeast.

The White Lady run (also signposted A' Bhaintighearna Bhan in Gaelic) is the main descent when you turn left out of the funicular's top station and ski down around the building's face towards the train line's mid-station. There's snow-fencing and an elevated track to your left and the raised moorland of the unpisted East Wall to your right. This latter area might be snow-covered, or rocks and heather may be visible. Ahead is a spectacular view across the Spey Valley and the Scottish Highlands over a vast vista to the west.

Graded red on the map, it's a moderately challenging, fairly straight descent that can be tackled by early intermediates or taken at speed by more experienced skiers and boarders. Below the mid-station there's a choice of easy runs back to the ski area's base where you can hop on the funicular or take one of the drag lifts over to the Coire Cas sector.

The run was one of the first in the country to be accessed by lifts, with the White Lady chairlift opening on 23 December 1961, following a route now occupied by the upper section of the funicular. Originally skiers hiked 15 kilometres (9 miles) cross country from Aviemore carrying their skis, then up the mountain to earn their turns. The lift was unique, it's claimed, in that skiers sat in pairs facing sideways as they ascended the hill. The lift marked the start of a golden era in Scottish skiing, particularly for Aviemore. It attracted the celebrities of the day and many hundreds of thousands of skiers each winter in an

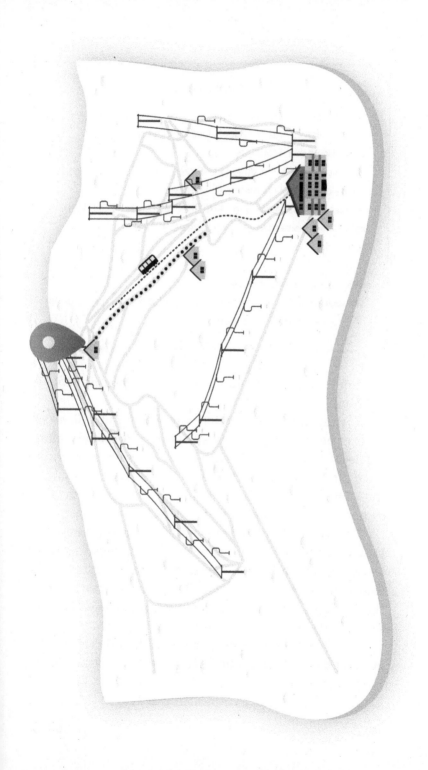

FACT FILE

IN SHORT The classic run of Scottish skiing that has witnessed the full history of that nation's love of snow sports.

DIFFICULTY OF RUN Moderate

VERTICAL OF RUN 335 metres (1,099 feet)

LENGTH OF RUN 1.2 kilometres (0.75 miles)

SKI AREA ALTITUDE RANGE 640–1,097 metres (2,100–3,600 feet)

RESORT AREA DIMENSIONS 30 kilometres (19 miles)

RUNS 31

LIFTS 12

WEB cairngormmountain.co.uk

GETTING THERE Rail to Aviemore, 15.5 kilometres (9.5 miles); or Air to Inverness, 77 kilometres (48 miles)

era before fast roads and cheap flights were available to the Alps.

Opening a few years before the White Lady, Glencoe's lift over on the west coast was the first in Scotland, ending the local tradition of hiking up to ski that had existed since the 1890s. But the White Lady was the first commercial venture, and by the end of the decade a victim of its own success with queues an hour long.

The White Lady snowfield was originally known as Lady Grant after the Grants of Rothiemurchus, the major landowners in the region. Her skirt is now dissected by the funicular railway line, which she appears a little disgruntled about since when the snow is deep, she sometimes sends drifts over the elevated track.

Despite the impact of climate change, there can still be great days on the White Lady and other Scottish slopes.

The snow arrives erratically so there may be skiing at Halloween one year or in June the next, but then another year it can be too warm for the lifts to open in January and February. All five Scottish centres now have 'all-weather' snowmaking machines, which (unlike most) can make snow even when it is +10°or 20°C (+50 or 68°F), and means they can at least open a limited amount of terrain even when Mother Nature refuses to play ball.

Keep an eye on the forecast and you might get lucky, or book months ahead but be prepared to switch to mountain biking or golf, perhaps with a tour of Loch Ness, Balmoral, a whisky distillery or two, and maybe some dolphin spotting in the Moray Firth. Whether you ski or not, you can always drink a bottle of White Lady beer produced by the local Cairngorm Brewery – a wheat beer that they first produced in 2011, to celebrate 50 years since the ski lift was installed at Cairngorm.

INGEMARBACKEN, TÄRNABY

SWEDEN

You can be forgiven if you've never heard of Tärnaby, a small community in Swedish Lapland, with a population of less than 500. But it is the home village of (Jan) Ingemar Stenmark, the man who dominated Alpine ski racing from the mid-1970s to the end of the 1980s, specialising in the technical slalom disciplines. Although American ski racer Mikaela Shiffrin appears to be closing in on his tally more than three decades later, Stenmark's 86 World Cup wins remain the greatest in the history of ski racing.

Tärnaby's ski area is, like the village, modest. There are five lifts, most of them drags, each running up from the valley floor. Stenmark's fame is such that not only does he have a ski run named after him, an honour several other all-time great racers have achieved, but also a ski lift. It's not a fancy lift either, but a good old T Bar that's the staple lift of Scandinavia, resistant to the frequent windy conditions.

Turn right off the top of the Ingemarliften and you are at the top of Stenmark's run, marked number 10 on the map. Its most intimidating section, graded black, comes immediately, but the slope does ease to red grade about a quarter of the way down. It goes pretty much straight down to the base of the ski area, which stretches alongside the large frozen lake Gäuta. So much of the pleasure of the descent comes in knowing that this is the slope where Ingemar and other great skiers learned their craft. In fact, this slope can claim to have inspired more World Cup wins than any other of the tens of thousands of ski slopes on Earth.

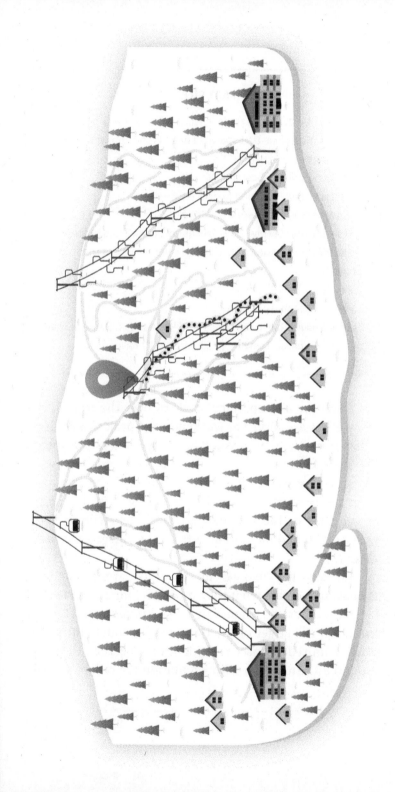

FACT FILE

IN SHORT It may not be the longest of ski runs or a famous resort but it's a slope that spawned more World Cup wins than any other.

DIFFICULTY OF RUN Moderate–Difficult

VERTICAL OF RUN 157 metres (515 feet)

LENGTH OF RUN 750 metres (2,460 feet)

SKI AREA ALTITUDE RANGE 439–789 metres (1,440–2,589 feet)

RESORT AREA DIMENSIONS 20 kilometres (13 miles)

RUNS 50

LIFTS 5

WEB hemavantarnaby.com

GETTING THERE Rail to Mo i Rana, 117 kilometres (73 miles); or Air to Hemavan Tärnaby, 19 kilometres (12 miles)

There are also spectacular views over the frozen lake, and waffles are served at weekends and peak season in the Fikastugan hut which you'll see to your left, just before the slope eases. It stays open as a 'warming hut' when not serving waffles, a much-needed haven when temperatures dip to double digits below freezing. Café Tärningen, at the base of the run next to the Ingemarliften, has a wider menu and memorabilia from the village's ski racing heroes.

Tärnaby has teamed up with its larger neighbour Hemavan to create what they proclaim 'northern Sweden's largest ski resort'. Hemavan is 18 kilometres (11 miles) away and the larger of the two, with a gondola lift and its much-admired Kobåset freeride area. Together they offer around 50 runs and a joint reputation for reliable powder snow, thanks to the northerly latitude. You also have a good chance of seeing the auroras when you visit.

Even without Hemavan, little Tärnaby has more strings to its bow. Ingemar began learning to race here at the age of five in the early 1960s, and went on to transcend his formidable skiing reputation to become recognised as one of the greatest Scandinavian athletes of all time, alongside Björn Borg in tennis. Remarkably, he's not the only big name to come out of this tiny town.

You can also ride the Anjaliften run, named after local girl Anja Pärson, who is another greatest-of-all-time with 42 World Cup wins between 1999 and 2012. Of the thousands of racers that have competed on the World Cup tour over the past five decades, her 42 wins places her 11th in the all-time list, 6th on the women's list. Like Stenmark she competed in three Winter Olympics, taking slalom gold in Turin. Unlike him she also excelled in the speed disciplines, taking Olympic medals in these too and winning the World Cup tour in the downhill, Super G and combined in 2007. Her incredible range of skills are reflected in the fact that the Anjabacken piste, number 15 to the right of the map, is one of the most complex on the mountain. Beginning black, it levels off to a blue midway before steepening again to a red down to the lakeshore.

Few if any ski resorts can match the number of World Cup wins and Olympic medals won by Tärnaby's Tärna IK Fjällvinden ski club, which can trace its history back to 1928. Besides Anja and Ingemar, there have been other World Cup winners, Stig Strand and most recently Jens Byggmark. It must be something in the air, or perhaps the snow of Tärnaby? Whatever it is, if they breed many more of the world's greatest skiers, they're going to need some more lifts to name after them.

G2, LEVI

In some parts of the planet, such as Lapland in northern Finland, the annual tilting of the earth means the sun sets in mid-December and doesn't rise again until mid-January. Just how long it disappears for depends on how far north you are – sometime a few days, sometimes weeks or even months (see T Bar run, page 170).

This period of perpetual night (it's not a complete blackout; there are a few hours of pale grey light in the middle of the day as the sun skirts below the horizon from east to west) makes for a very different skiing experience. The region is famous for its light powder snow, which can fall for days on end in midwinter. Combined with the natural half-light, the mist of ever-falling snow makes skiing an ethereal, dream-like experience.

Levi's G2 slope hosts World Cup ski racing in November each year, one of the first meetings of the season. In fact, the resort uses snow farming – storing large amounts of snow undercover through the summer, then spreading it out to create a ski run when temperatures cool again in the autumn – to open for its seven-month ski season at the start of October.

Apart from hosting World Cup races, G2 is also one of Finland's steepest slopes at a 52 per cent pitch, and continues for a satisfying 1.5 kilometre (just under a mile) descent. It's also one of the few served by a gondola lift, a nice, fast, modern one at that. G2 is reached from the top of the World Cup gondola, the area's highest point. It's up above the treeline, with forests stretching out in many

FACT FILE

IN SHORT Santa, the Northern Lights, World Cup racing? Lapland has got it all, and you can even ski or board here once the sun has disappeared under the horizon for a while around the winter solstice.

DIFFICULTY OF RUN Moderate

VERTICAL OF RUN 325 metres (1,066 feet)

LENGTH OF RUN 1.5 kilometres (0.9 mile)

SKI AREA ALTITUDE RANGE 200–531 metres (656–1,742 feet)

RESORT AREA DIMENSIONS 40 kilometres (25 miles)

RUNS 43

LIFTS 27

WEB levi.fi

GETTING THERE Rail to Kolari, 85 kilometres (53 miles); or Air to Kittilä, 15 kilometres (9 miles)

directions and, if you look north, very few people between you and the North Pole.

Run G2 widens and steepens, and becomes the stretch where the gradient of 52 per cent provides a sudden challenge to World Cup racers. With the gondola waiting for you to go back up, it's tempting to just do laps. If you're there on a cold day (and temperatures well into double-digits below freezing are the norm in midwinter), the gondola cabins also provide a chance to warm up a bit.

Of course, Lapland in December is much more famous for two other things beside its skiing: Santa and the Northern Lights. Skiers are likely to be one in perhaps 100 people arriving to the area. Everyone else is here to meet Santa (always entertaining to see people arriving from mainland European cities who are completely unprepared for an Arctic winter) and hopefully to see the aurora.

The Santa visits vary greatly, and although children are usually too excited to notice the difference, their parents might. If you can afford the personal experience that some of Santa's more exclusive operations offer, that's usually best. The aurora, however, is available to all free of charge, and if you're really lucky you'll end up skiing under the Northern Lights. More likely, though, you'll spend your visit with that fine snow falling, meaning cloudy skies. It's a potluck.

Outside 'Santa season', Levi and other Lapland ski areas offer winter activities, including dog-sledding, snow-mobiling and reindeer safaris. As with your visit to Santa, the more you can afford, the more personalised your experience will be. Dog-sledding is a wonderful experience, and reindeer farming is big in Lapland, with the best animals changing hands for huge sums, so it is fascinating to meet these beautiful creatures and learn more about their lives and herders. It's no surprise that Santa is such a fan.

By the end of the ski season in April and early May, Scandinavia's northern ski hills see near 24-hour daylight. As the cold weather lingers longer at these latitudes, the snow is often in better condition here at this time of the year than down in the Alps, making a return trip at the end of the season rather appealing.

Over the border in Sweden, the famous resort of Riks-gränsen has for years marketed itself as 'the spring skiing capital of Europe'. Located 200 kilometres (125 miles) north of the Arctic Circle, it only opens at the start of spring and by early May offers skiing/boarding under the mid-night sun. It closes in early June but reopens for a special Midsummer celebration, snow permitting, in late June.

T BAR RUN, NORDVÅGEN

NORWAY

It's a popular misconception that the Swedish resort of Riksgränsen is the world's most northerly ski area – though it does lie at 68°25'40"N, 200 kilometres (125 miles) within the Arctic Circle, where it's so cold and dark in midwinter that the ski season doesn't start until March and runs until June.

Some guess the Norwegian coastal town of Narvik must be the most northerly. It's reached by train, past Riksgränsen and across the border to the end of the line, and is in fact a tad further south at 68°25'14"N. The world's most northerly university city of Tromsø, at 69°40'58"N, also has a neat mid-sized ski area with fabulous views out over the local fjords.

Where truly is the most northerly ski area is a matter of definition. Just as you can argue that Gulmarg in India (at time of writing) has the world's highest-altitude lifts (reaching 3,950 metres/12,959 feet), you could also make the case for the gondola to Jade Dragon Snow Mountain in Lijiang, China, which reaches 4,700 metres (15,420 feet), but where skiing is virtually impossible now.

Similarly, there are ski lifts further north still than Tromsø. Actually, the very furthest north is on the Svalbard Islands at Longyearbyen, Spitzbergen, the world's most northerly community of more than 2,500 people. The lift here was originally a small 120-metre (394-feet) long tow, used mostly by local kids, but has recently been upgraded to a new 500-metre (1,640-feet) long lift, opening up much more vertical. It's at 78°13'N, so further north of our other

candidates. You might not book a ski holiday there, except to claim you've ridden the world's most northerly ski lift.

So our winner is the ski area at Nordvågen, population 440, which opened in 1985, the only proper ski area lying above 70 degrees north. It's in a spectacular location at Norway's (and Europe's) Northern Cape, at 70°58'49"N. There are even hotels.

'The world's northernmost ski resort!' confirm the volunteers that run Nordvågen ski area on their webpage, which also claims 'the lowest prices in the country'. These two facts alone make it worth the 700-kilometre (435-miles) road trip further north-east from Riksgränsen, but the fact that the drive is one of the world's most spectacular, along Norway's northern coast, makes it a firm fixture on every skier's bucket list.

Skiing at Nordvågen begins with an ascent on the area's modern T Bar lift, which is precisely 837 metres (2,746 feet) long and serves descents of about a kilometre (just over half a mile) in length and of intermediate difficulty. There are spectacular coastal views, which are a feature of much of the skiing here and in the surrounding region. It's a wide, circling run on open mountainside, skiing straight down towards the sea, starting gentle and with its steepest section in the middle. On high mountains the trees end at a certain altitude, but they also end at a certain latitude as you head north. In Europe that point is around 70 degrees, a little further north than most other parts of the Arctic Circle thanks to the influence of the warming North Atlantic Current.

Although the snow here is some of Europe's best, and usually reliable, the season is relatively short. The sun sets in Nordvågen in mid-November and doesn't reappear until 21 January, and that's about when the season begins.

FACT FILE

IN SHORT Skiing the world's most northerly ski area.

DIFFICULTY OF RUN Easy–Moderate

VERTICAL OF RUN 218 metres (715 feet)

LENGTH OF RUN 0.8 kilometres (0.5 miles)

SKI AREA ALTITUDE RANGE 13–231 metres (43–758 feet)

RESORT AREA DIMENSIONS 2 kilometres (1.25 miles)

RUNS 2

LIFTS 1

WEB nordkapp.no

GETTING THERE Rail to Narvik, 680 kilometres (423 miles); or Air to Honningsvåg, 9 kilometres (6 miles)

The run is fully floodlit, though, to offer night skiing. The volunteers run the area, grooming the slope and manning the lift, as well as a neat little base building complete with gear rental and coffee machine, until late April.

Of course, to make the most of your ski holiday on the North Cape, you'll be skiing the same run many times, but there are plenty of ways to alternate the descent, perhaps even dipping into the powder on the side.

Take a look at a map and you'll see there are other bits of land in the far north of the world that might just have a secret ski area. The tip of Scandinavia goes surprisingly far north, way above Iceland and more than halfway up Greenland. Svalbard lines up with the most northerly islands of North America and Russia as well as the northern tip of Greenland – all largely uninhabited.

Candidates that come close to Nordvågen include Greenland's Aasiaat, which Skiresort.info credits with a

115-metre (377-feet) vertical served by a single drag lift and a kilometre of slopes. It's at 68°42'35"N. Across Baffin Bay and all the way to Alaska, America's most northerly ski area is Skiland – Mount Aurora serving the city of Fairbanks at 64°50'37"N.

The Soviet Union used a carrot and stick approach for its massive mining operation; mining cities were created in the far north and people were enticed to move there by the offer of modern apartments and leisure activities like skiing. Most of these areas are now ghost towns, but the world's northernmost city with a population of more than 100,000 (around 175,000 in fact), Norilsk, does have a small ski hill with a T Bar. It's the second-largest city (after Murmansk) inside the Arctic Circle and lies at 69°20'N.

THE WOLF SLOPE (LUPULUI), POIANA BRAȘOV

ROMANIA

The Carpathian Mountains of Central Europe, particularly the area in the Transylvanian region of Romania, are closely associated with the tale of Count Dracula. Like most bitter and inhospitable storybook locations, however, they also turn out to be great for skiing.

Remarkably, Romania is (or perhaps more accurately 'was'), home to around 100 ski areas. The vast majority of these were rudimentary affairs with just a drag lift or two, dating from the socialist era, and many are likely now no more. The country does have several bigger, international destination ski areas too, including its best known, Poiana Brașov. Host to the skiing events at the 2013 European Youth Olympic Winter Festival, it's also conveniently close to what the Romanian Tourist Board have dubbed 'Dracula's Castle'.

The Wolf Slope, marked number one on the map and named Partia Lupului in Romanian, is the resort's most challenging. It descends almost the full vertical of the ski area, over nearly 3 kilometres (almost 2 miles). It's officially graded black, although most skiers of moderate ability can tackle it, as it would be at the steeper end of a red-/blue-square-graded run in some resorts.

Starting at the point where the small area of open mountainside above the treeline ends, the run begins wide and moderately steep, before steepening and narrowing as you descend. You're surrounded by thick forest on either side of the descent for almost its entire length.

Snow conditions can add to the challenge of the slope if the run gets icy, which is fairly common. The snowfall here usually arrives and then departs a little earlier than in the Alps, with the best conditions normally from December through to February, and starting to thaw from late spring.

Although Poiana Brașov is of modest scale, good skiers will find guides happy to take them touring in the wider area of the Carpathians, considered an under-rated gem by its fans. The ski area was marketed as 'cheap and cheerful' in the latter decades of the twentieth century, but while it remains one of the more affordable in Europe, the downside was the long queues at the aged lifts. There has been investment into a nice new gondola and fast quad and six-seat chairlifts in more recent times. The latter two take you out from the base of Lupului and deliver you to the top of the run, respectively.

The ski resort lies 15 kilometres (9 miles) from the charming old city of Brașov, which, with a population of a quarter of a million, is Romania's seventh biggest. It's a university city full of characterful and affordable shops, bars and restaurants and well worth a visit. Sights not to miss include Strada Sforii or 'Rope Street', known as Romania's and one of Europe's narrowest at 111 centimetres (44 inches) and mentioned in documents dating back as far as the seventeenth century. The imposing Black Church helps build the Gothic romance of the region, but the belief that it was blackened in a city fire of 1689 has now been discredited in favour of the theory that the blackening happened due to the less dramatic cause of industrial pollution two centuries later.

Of course, no visit to Poiana Brașov is complete without

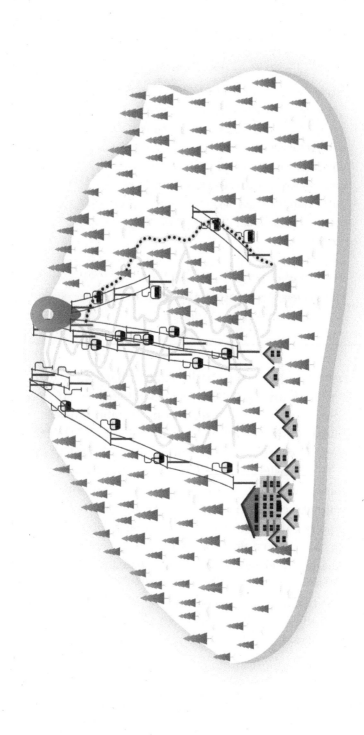

FACT FILE

IN SHORT Count Dracula probably never visited here but there's an impressive castle nearby that fits Bram Stoker's spec, so let's go skiing in Transylvania. It's just a jump to the left.

DIFFICULTY OF RUN Difficult

VERTICAL OF RUN 728 metres (2,388 feet)

LENGTH OF RUN 2,860 metres (9,383 feet))

SKI AREA ALTITUDE RANGE 941–1,783 metres (3,087–5,850 feet)

RESORT AREA DIMENSIONS 24 kilometres (15 miles)

RUNS 12

LIFTS 11

WEB discoverpoiana.ro

GETTING THERE Rail to Râșnov, 11 kilometres (7 miles); or Air to Brașov, 21 kilometres (13 miles)

---

a day trip to Dracula's Castle. Except that, sadly, it probably isn't. Bran Castle, located 25 kilometres (16 miles) south-west of the ski resort looks suitably austere and intimidating. It also dates back to at least the thirteenth century, a century or so before Vlad III Dracula (aka Vlad The Impaler), whose name Stoker borrowed for his character, was born. In the 1970s, as the hard-up socialist government of Romania sought Western currency, someone spotted that cheap ski holidays with Dracula's castle on the doorstep could be a big draw.

There's no evidence that Stoker had any knowledge of Bran Castle, and the castle he describes does not resemble it. Vlad the Impaler is never known to have set foot in it, but we will skip lightly over these details so as not to spoil this holiday highlight.

Excitingly, Transylvania is also home to Europe's highest number of fortified churches, again many dating from Vlad III Dracula's time. It turns out they were strengthened to fend off invading Ottomans and Tatars, however, not vampires.

1931 ROUTE, MOUNT OLYMPUS

GREECE

Many people don't realise that Mount Olympus, home to the Gods in the Greek myths, is a real place. Fewer still know that you can ski on it.

It is big; its highest point rises to 2,917 metres (9,570 feet). That may be 1,900 metres (6,234 feet) lower than Mont Blanc, but while most of Europe's highest mountains rise out of the already high ground, Olympus rises from near sea level and has a prominence of 2,353 metres (7,720 feet), with no other mountain of similar height for 250 kilometres (156 miles). In ancient times, Homer believed the mountain's peaks pierced the sky.

Those who make it to the top are rewarded by stunning views out over the Aegean Sea, just 17 kilometres (10 miles) away and much of Greece. It's a great spot for a god to build a palace. The legends talk of Zeus having a large palace complex at the mountain's highest point, Mytikas ('Pantheon' in the myths). This had a very large courtyard in front which was big enough to house all the Greek gods (besides the dozen who lived permanently on Olympus, there were many thousands more). Olympus actually has 51 other separate peaks, all a little lower than Mytikas, so space wouldn't have been a problem.

Above 2,000 metres Olympus is snow-capped from around September to May, and drifting can cause the snow to reach 8–10 metres (26–33 feet) thick in places, with average winter temperatures –5°C. That said, there was a Greek Goddess of snow, Chione, a daughter of Boreas, God of the wintry north wind, so she might have been a help.

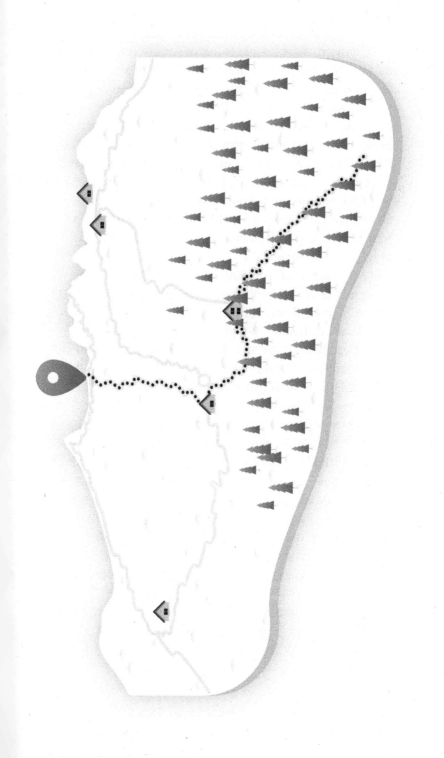

Of course, most people think of Greece for its sunshine and beaches, but in fact, more than half of the country is classified as mountainous (that's the highest percentage of any country in the EU). It is also home to around two dozen ski areas, the largest of which, Mount Parnassos, has more than 35 kilometres (22 miles) of runs, served by 17 lifts. The ski area on Mount Olympus is at the other end of the scale, though: it's very small with just three simple drag lifts and about 5 kilometres (3 miles) of fairly easy runs located at the end of a dirt road. (Don't mix it up with Mount Olympus ski area in New Zealand, marketed as, 'the playground of the gods'.)

The centre, at a point called Vrysopoules on the western side of the mountain, has been managed by the KEOAX (Greek Army) since 1961, and while the Greek public are welcome, it's only open at weekends from December through to March. On the upside, if you have Greek national ID you can use the lifts for free. Due to the usual military sensitivities, foreigners need to obtain special permission to ski here from the Special Forces Directorate of Hellenic Army General Staff.

Since the 1930s, skiers have been ascending the slopes on foot with skins beneath their skis to stop them sliding back as they climb. The first ascent of Olympus with a descent by skis was made by a group of three French and Greek skiers and mountaineers on 20 March 1931, and the route they took is still followed today. Gustave Dorier, Kostas Natsis and Iraklis Ioannidis spent the morning skinning up the mountain's gentle western slopes, reaching one of the many lower summits, Skala (2,882 metres / 9,455 feet) around noon. Switching from skis to crampons, they followed the ridge from here to the main summit, roped together. With stretches of soft snow and ice, this

FACT FILE

IN SHORT Skiing from Zeus's palace on the mountain of the gods.

DIFFICULTY OF RUN Difficult–Expert

VERTICAL OF RUN 1,250 metres (4,101 feet)

LENGTH OF RUN 5 kilometres (3 miles)

SKI AREA ALTITUDE RANGE 1,000–2,917 metres (3,281–9,570 feet)

RESORT AREA DIMENSIONS 5 kilometres (3 miles)

LIFTS 3

WEB wayoutadventures.gr / olympusfd.gr / visit-olympus.travel

GETTING THERE Rail to Litochoro, 18 kilometres (10 miles); or Air to Thessaloniki, 109 kilometres (89 miles)

section was hard going and it was late afternoon when they reached Zeus's home. After taking in the immensity of their achievement, the three returned to Skala and began a ski descent of nearly 2,000 vertical metres (6,262 feet) to round off a very long but no doubt incredibly satisfying day.

It was nearly seven decades before ski touring on Olympus really began to take off in the late 1990s, however. Ski mountaineers from around the world began to arrive, reportedly stunned by the scale and challenge. Among them was the late Davo Karničar, the Slovenian skier who was the first person to make a complete ski descent from the highest peaks on all seven continents, including the first to ski down from the summit of Everest in 2000.

Karničar recreated the ascent via Skala, then the ridge walk, but this time followed by a descent of a 45-degree couloir on the side of Mytikas, heading down to a small mountain refuge called Christos Kakkalos (named after the first man known to have reached the summit of Olympus), located about 1,250 vertical metres (4,101 feet) below on the Plateau of the Muses.

Olympus is popular as it lacks glacial dangers like crevasses, but its full snow-covered vertical is reserved for fit and highly skilled ski mountaineers who can handle the steep terrain up high, both ascending and descending.

Your other option to ski or board the mountain of the gods, if you have the funds, is a helicopter. For those who can live with (or offset) their carbon footprint, the heliski options are spectacular. Heliski Adventures Worldwide began operating trips in the region in 2012 and a few years later provided the logistics and guides for the Warren Miller Entertainment's ski flick *No Turning Back* (2014). One of the heliski pioneers in the region, Craig Calonica, a member of the US Speed Skiing Team in the 1970s and 80s who went on to ski mountaineer and heliski around the world, also opened up heliskiing on and around Mount Everest.

Incidentally, some scholars have speculated that the name 'Olympus' originally meant 'mountain' in the language of a pre-Greek civilisation, so perhaps you're skiing on the first mountain named a mountain?

PRIUT TO AZAU, MOUNT ELBRUS

RUSSIA

The jury is out as to which is Europe's highest mountain. There's a strong school of thought, especially among the French and Italians, that Mont Blanc (4,808 metres/15,774 feet) on the Franco-Italian border is top dog. However, the mountain skiers wishing to tick off the highest peak on each continent look to the other side of the European continental plate. Russia's Mount Elbrus, 2,800 kilometres (1,740 miles) to the east, is a twin-topped dormant volcano, towering 5,642 metres (18,510 feet) up in the Caucasus Mountains, more than 800 metres (2,624 feet) higher than Mont Blanc. Even the frequent tweaking of the precise height of the two peaks after summit snow accumulates or thaws away won't change the winner for aeons yet.

Elbrus rises majestically from high green plains stretching northward, with the Caspian Sea to the east and the Black Sea, the region that hosted the 2014 Winter Olympics at Sochi, to the west. For climbers, it is, despite its greater height, a less technical challenge than Mont Blanc. The main threats include very strong winds, glacial crevasses, falling rocks, avalanches and altitude sickness. It has a series of modern gondola lifts and an optional snowcat ride from the top of the highest lift, taking you to within 1,000 vertical metres (3,281 feet) of the top. Mont Blanc is easier to get to, but there are no lifts on it.

For skiers, those lifts open up one of the world's greatest lift-served verticals from one of the planet's highest lift-served points. We're talking 1,500 vertical metres (4,921 feet) using the lifts, 2,300 vertical metres (7,546 feet) if you take the snowcat. If you're really fit and hardcore, you can ski around 3,300 vertical metres (10,827 feet) from the top to the bottom.

For most, this descent begins at 4,050 metres (13,287 feet) at Priut, served by snowcat or a hike up from the top of the lifts. From Priut to Garabashi at the top of the lifts, it's a fairly tame gradient as the glacier ends and you hit the mountainside beneath the ice. At this point you are on to the steepest inbound terrain, beginning with red run 7 which pops under the gondola line to skier's right then follows it down to the mid-station at 3,500 metres (11,483 feet) at Mir (or 'Peace', you remember the space station?). Above and below Mir station you are on the open mountainside, with the run in a natural wide valley for much of its length, so you can bounce off the sides if you wish for added fun.

Run 4 merges into a third red, number 2, as the natural valley sweeps to skier's left and you follow the line of the bottom lift down from Horizon at 3,000 metres (9,843 feet) to the base of the ski area mountain at Azau. It's worth noting that at 2,350 metres (7,710 feet), this is one of the highest resort bases anywhere in the world outside of Colorado. Everything is above the treeline and, of course, at these altitudes you can expect the snow to be good. The season generally lasts into May and sometimes makes it into June.

What used to be the main problem with Elbrus – aged cable cars and a shaky power supply, making lift operation problematic – is rarely an issue today. The past decade has seen the resort transform under the auspices of the Resorts of the North Caucasus which has invested over a billion roubles and keeps spending.

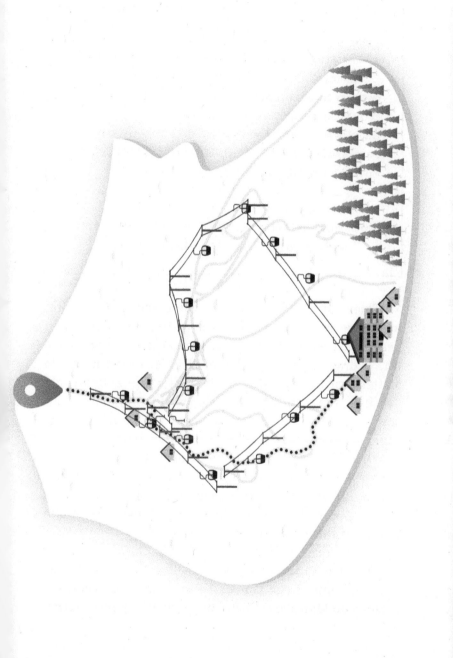

Skiers also love to debate where the highest point in Europe is that you can reach with a lift, rather than needing climbing skills or a helicopter. The highest fixed lift, a drag, is on top of the Klein Matterhorn at the Matterhorn Paradise glacier ski area above Zermatt and Cervinia. The point known as Gobba di Rollin that the lift reaches is also the starting point of the new FIS World Cup cross-border ski run down into Italy. The lift reaches 3,899 metres (12,792 feet), but unusually it isn't open in the winter season, only from spring to autumn. The highest winter lift at Zermatt is a shade lower at 3,883 metres (12,739 feet), which is still higher than anywhere else in Europe at this time of year.

Second place is more open to debate. One candidate, at 3,842 metres (12,605 feet) is Mont Blanc's neighbour and starting point of the famous Vallée Blanche descent, the Aiguille du Midi above Chamonix. Pedantics point out that

Aiguille du Midi's top station is multi-storey and the listed height refers to the top floor, but the cable car actually comes in at the base. Do you include the elevator within the building in the total height, especially when there's quite a few vertical metres to shuffle down to the top of the run proper (see Vallée Blanche, page 79)? That said, the run has been skied from the building itself down the *arête* by several daredevils over the years; most but not all lived to tell the tale.

With all those provisos, Mount Elbrus probably has the stronger claim. Its piste map shows its highest gondola climbing to 3,847 metres (12,621 feet), a few metres higher than the top of the Aiguille du Midi, and, of course, you ski straight out of the top.

Mount Elbrus could settle the matter once and for all if they ever build a long-planned lift up to Priut at 4,050 metres (13,287 feet), making it not just the highest lift-served area in Europe but the whole world, overtaking Gulmarg in India (so long as we ignore the already mentioned even higher gondola in China for not being a 'proper' ski resort). If you consider a snowcat a lift, Mount Elbrus can already claim second place, as its snowcat goes to around 4,600 metres (15,092 feet) from the top of the highest gondola.

Fortunately, we are down in the 3,500 metres (11,483 feet) altitude range for those in fourth place or below (Saas-Fee, La Grave, Les 2 Alpes) so the debate ends there.

MALUTI, AFRISKI

LESOTHO

A single-kilometre-long, and not especially steep, piste may not seem like a 'must ski' for your bucket list. However, this is the closest outdoor snow slope to the equator, and there's no major ski area in any direction for at least 8,000 kilometres (approximately 5,000 miles), so the residents of the landlocked mountainous kingdom of Lesotho, and their South African neighbours in Johannesburg, are very happy to have it.

Afriski is one of the world's newer ski areas and one of the highest. First opened in 2000, it is located 3,050 metres (10,007 feet) above sea level in the Maluti Mountains. Despite being only around 3,200 kilometres (2,000 miles) from the equator, that kind of altitude means it is almost always close to freezing here from late May to August. Afriski's operators are skilled snowmakers, so they create the main slope, along with a beginners' run, several terrain parks and other snowy attractions with machines in May and the snow lasts all winter. In fact, it is often one of the first, and sometimes the very first, in the southern hemisphere to open for the season, ahead of ski areas in the Andes, Australia and New Zealand.

There can, and usually is, natural snowfall too, several times each season. The trick is to be already at the area when the snow arrives because it makes the access roads tricky. These snowfalls are few and far between, as sunshine is the predominant weather, and most will find they are skiing or boarding a ribbon of white surrounded by grassy high Alpine terrain.

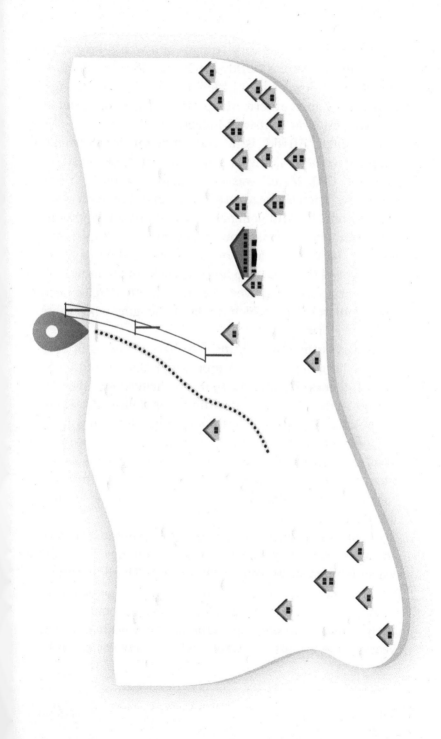

The Main Slope is very straight and would be graded blue at most ski areas worldwide. It's usually quiet so most skiers whizz down, gleeful they're skiing where very few people have in southern Africa! Then it's on to refuel at the Sky Restaurant, Africa's highest.

Although Afriski is a very modern development, people have been skiing in southern Africa for a century or more. Club Maluti was established in 1968 by a few university friends, negotiating the land use with local tribal chiefs. It's still going and located just a few kilometres from where Afriski now stands, but is a simpler, less commercial venture. Most of the skiers heading to either centre travel the four or so hours drive from Johannesburg or Pretoria, crossing over the 3,222-metre (10,571-feet) high Mahlasela Pass, which can be challenging when there is a snowstorm.

Africa is the only continent to have ski areas in both the northern hemisphere (Morocco and Algeria, and if you count indoors, Egypt) and southern hemisphere (besides Afriski there is a centre at Tiffindell in South Africa, but at the time of writing it has not operated for two winters through the pandemic and it is unclear if it will reopen). That means you can enjoy winter skiing in Africa for six months of the year if you're prepared to travel. There are so few ski areas with lifts here that they can be counted on one hand.

South Africa also has an unusual place in the history of the machines that make snow in any conditions, including warm temperatures well above freezing. These machines, which make their 'snow' within a large refrigerated unit ready to spread out on the slopes, have become increasingly popular in ski areas around the world in recent years. Some are used at resorts where snow cover can be

problematic, such as Scottish centres, to guarantee there's
at least some snow; others are used to ensure snow at
skiing or snowboarding competitions, where it's needed
for the athletes and TV crews. Back in the 1990s, an Israeli
company, IDE Technologies, sold a machine designed to
cool temperatures far underground to a South African gold
mine. Unexpectedly, the machine started churning rather
nice snow out under the hot South African sunshine above
ground as a by-product of the cooling process. Eventually,
someone thought this was something that might be sold
to ski resorts in a warming world, and in the early nough-
ties the rebranded 'IDE Snowmaker' machines were sold
to several resorts in the Alps, including the Pitztal and
Zermatt glaciers in Austria and Switzerland respectively,
to ensure snow cover in late summer and early autumn

---

when they are among the few northern hemisphere ski areas operating.

Africa is also home to some of the closest snowfields to the equator, in countries like Kenya, Tanzania and Uganda. Most of these have been skied at some point by adventurers like self-confessed 'ski bum' Jimmy Petterson in his quest to ski every country possible around the world (documented in his magnum opus *Skiing Around the World*, volumes I and II). Jimmy recounts hiking and climbing for days through the jungle, carrying his skis, to make a few turns on short old patches of snow 5,000 metres (16,404 feet) up. Sadly, these remaining snow patches are fast disappearing so Jimmy may have been among the last to ski them.

RUN 3, MOUNT HERMON

ISRAEL

Along with seas and oceans, mountain ranges tend to be the natural borders between regions, countries and continents. Given that most countries grew up when both were difficult to cross, that's no real surprise. Yet it always feels good when ski lifts and runs cross these artificial lines. For example, in 2009 a cable car and piste were built to connect ski areas on the Italian and Slovenian sides of the border through what was once the Iron Curtain; whatever the political doctrine, the free-thinking and universal language of the mountains won through.

But their border locations sometimes turn mountains into battlefields of either full-on conflict or guerrilla wars of attrition. In the former category, the Dinaric Alps between Croatia and Bosnia and Herzegovina, which saw the 1984 Olympic Games staged at Sarajevo a decade or so before, became a battleground in the Bosnian Wars. Similarly, the Himalayan mountains of Kashmir have seen border skirmishes between India and Pakistan, who dispute ownership of the territory.

The Golan Heights, currently largely in Israel, have changed hands between different nations and religions down through the millennia more times than almost anywhere else on earth. The Bible talks of the Philistines building shrines to their gods there, then Greek, then Roman command by the time that Jesus Christ visited. It was here, some scholars speculate, that the Biblical 'Transfiguration' took place, an episode when Jesus took three of his disciples, Peter, James and John, up a mountain where Old Testament characters Moses and Elijah appeared and Jesus himself became dazzlingly bright.

Most recently, Israel annexed about two-thirds of the strategically important Heights from Syria during the Six-Day War in 1967, a move that UN Security Council Resolution 497 still declares null and void.

Israel then built a ski resort on the Golan Heights, the country's only one. Mount Hermon ski area is located on the south-east facing slopes of the Heights, just a few kilometres from the so-called 'Purple Line', which marks the de-facto border between Israel and Syria. The first ski lift was installed not long after annexation in 1971, but the ski area really began to grow a decade later, and today there are 10 lifts serving about 45 kilometres (28 miles) of runs spread over 243 hectares (600 acres) for all ability levels.

Of course, the ongoing religious, political, diplomatic and military conflict in the Middle East means that skiing Mount Hermon is not your typical ski day. If you look on a map you'll see that the captured land on which the ski area is located sticks out to form Israel's northern tip, a thin strip of land with Lebanon to the west, Syria to the east. It's believed to be the only ski area located within an active military site. Bags are checked as you arrive, soldiers armed with automatic weapons man lift stations, an Israeli Army lookout post sits on the slopes, and if you make a wrong turn off the lift you might inadvertently ski into closed military land. But the rumours of off-piste land mines are reported to be fantasy. Well, so long as you don't ski too far from the slopes.

An estimated 300,000 Israelis battle their way up through chronic traffic congestion on the one road each season, many of them just to see snow, only two hours

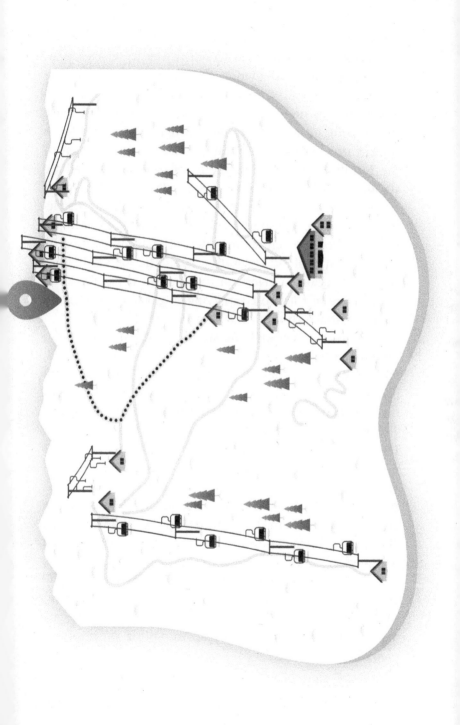

from the desert. Plenty learn to ski on Mount Hermon and around 50,000 Israelis head off to the Alps to ski each year.

A newly installed gondola lifts skiers to the top of the slopes from where, on a clear day, there are fabulous views down towards the Sea of Galilee, 96 kilometres (60 miles) to the south (the River Jordan, which runs down to it, springs up in these mountains). In skiing terms, most of the terrain is quite monotonous, of easy-to-intermediate standard. With little tree cover you can ski or board almost everywhere, always keeping in mind those military restrictions. There are two short black runs and two of the slopes have also been recognised for international competition by the International Ski Federation (FIS). The long red run 3 (with the option to divert on to 3A or 3B if you're skiing laps) is one of the most satisfying, a glorious long cruise sweeping down through the heart of the ski area.

In the early decades the snow was usually best from January to March, but as with ski areas across the world, climate change is having an impact here too, and there are occasionally winters now with no snow at all. There's no snowmaking on Mount Hermon and 2017–18 saw a 13-day season. In these poorer winters, snowfall is most likely in late January or February. Of course, the capricious nature of global warming can mean unexpected dumps of snow outside the usual season. In early December 2010, for example, a huge 1.5-metre (5-foot) snowfall led to the centre opening more than a month earlier than expected. Not quite so early, but a similar storm hit in 2015 – when it's good, it's good.

While Israel controls part of the mountain, Syria still runs a higher part of it to the east, peaking at 2,814 metres (9,232 feet). In 2005, six years before Syria's civil war began, a story emerged of a Syrian plan to build a ski resort on

FACT FILE

IN SHORT Hermon is a mountain that appears in stories back to antiquity; some believe Jesus himself visited here. Israel have built a ski resort on the part of the mountain it controls.

DIFFICULTY OF RUN Moderate

VERTICAL OF RUN 440 metres (1,444 feet)

LENGTH OF RUN 3 kilometres (1.9 miles)

SKI AREA ALTITUDE RANGE 1,600–2,040 metres (5,249–6,693 feet)

RESORT AREA DIMENSIONS 243 hectares (600 acres)

RUNS 45 kilometres (28 miles)

LIFTS 10

WEB skihermon.co.il

GETTING THERE Rail to Karmiel, 95 kilometres (59 miles); or Air to Tel Aviv, 169 kilometres (105 miles)

their part of the mountain. This wasn't going to be any old ski area, though; this one had an incredible $15 billion price tag with investment coming from Kuwait and Saudi Arabia. There was clearly no point starting small. The project was due to take 15 years to complete but sadly is yet to commence.

KORNET, THE CEDARS

LEBANON

Lebanon is probably not your first thought when planning your ski holiday, but there are half-a-dozen ski areas on snow-capped mountains that rise up quickly from sea level to the highest peak at 3,088 metres (10,131 feet). Indeed, this is one place where you can be skiing fresh snow one minute then swimming in a warm sea less than an hour later, or vice versa, so long as you can beat Lebanon's notoriously chaotic traffic.

Despite Lebanon's reputation as a hot, dry country, people have been skiing here for over a century. The first recorded Lebanese skier was a student returning from his studies in Switzerland in 1913, who introduced skiing to his friends upon his return. Two decades later, the country's first ski club was established to encourage participation, and shortly afterwards the first ski school. Lebanon's first ski lift began operating in 1953.

That ski school was established at what became Lebanon's first ski resort, The Cedars, by the French Army, which was essentially running the country at the time. There is quite a pattern of military involvement in ski area development in the Middle East as well as other nations in Western Asia, in part because soldiers patrol the mountains that form borders (in this case with Syria). The exciting winter sport of biathlon – which involves endurance, high-speed cross-country skiing, then stopping and being calm enough to fire a rifle to hit tiny distant targets on a shooting range – grew out of military exercises.

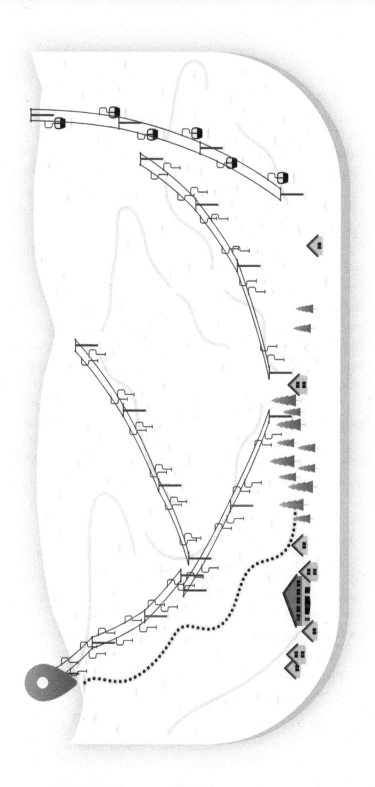

The road up to The Cedars begins to climb initially through terraced vineyards before you reach open (hopefully snow-covered) hillside. When you near the resort itself the first thing you will notice are the magnificent cedar trees after which it is named. The cedar is highly significant to Lebanon; it's the country's national emblem and, like forests the world over, was once much more extensive. Sometimes referred to as 'The Cedars of God', the trees are mentioned in the Old Testament in the Psalms of King David and are referenced in many other cultures dating back to the ancient Egyptians, who noted how good they were for shipbuilding. Even more ancient Sumerians record them as a meriting protection from their god Enlil. Over millennia, human activity and now climate change have taken their toll, but the trees still look magnificent. From the fifteenth century right up to today, tourists continue to rave about them.

The ski slopes themselves, however, are on the open mountainside above the treeline. This is not Lebanon's largest ski area, but there are half-a-dozen lifts including several quad chairs. The resort also boasts Lebanon's highest lift-served point and its biggest vertical. With the ski area's base at nearly 2,100 metres (6,890 feet) altitude, it has a reputation for the country's best snow quality and longest season.

Most of the ski runs are located within a huge basin that funnels skiers, on-piste and off, down to the base. The easier terrain is largely located to the right of the slopes as you ascend. Our descent is off to the left, taking the quad and then jumping on the sole double chair at the top to make it up to the top of the slopes at Kornet for the maximum vertical descent.

```
┌─────────────────────────────────────────────────┐
│                   FACT FILE                       │
│                                                   │
│  IN SHORT  Skiing in the morning then swimming in the Med in the │
│           warm waters of the Middle East is all the more special with │
│           the stunning Cedars of Lebanon in sight. │
│  DIFFICULTY OF RUN  Moderate                       │
│  VERTICAL OF RUN  750 metres (2,461 feet)          │
│  LENGTH OF RUN  2.4 kilometres (1.5 miles)         │
│  SKI AREA ALTITUDE RANGE  2,100–2,850 metres (6,890–9,350 feet) │
│  RESORT AREA DIMENSIONS  9 kilometres (5.5 miles)  │
│  LIFTS  7                                          │
│  WEB  facebook.com/teleskiscedarsslopes           │
│  GETTING THERE  Air to Beirut, 142 kilometres (88 miles) │
│                                                   │
└─────────────────────────────────────────────────┘
```

All of the terrain dropping down from Kornet is rated black, but our run takes us to skier's left and a slightly gentler descent out above the resort, opening up magnificent views of the wide region below. Travel up to Pic des Dames (2,650 metres/8,694 feet) for a choice of two more black-graded descents, this time with a gully between two outcrops which provides more varied terrain to bounce off, and if you're really lucky a bit of a powder stash.

In 1941 Lebanon and Syria became a focus of battle in World War II, with the Nazis using their puppet Vichy Government in France to try to control the wider region. On 8 June 1941, the Allies sent in a force of 20,000 Australian, Indian, Free French and British troops to take control. One of these was a gentleman called Jimmy Riddell, who, in 1929, cut nearly half an hour off the then best time for the famous Inferno race at Mürren, Switzerland, first staged the year before and still going strong today. The winners are still awarded a James Riddell memorial medal to this day.

Riddell was based in Homs, in Western Syria, when an enquiry arrived from HQ, reportedly on a particularly hot and sultry evening during a sandstorm, asking whether anyone had skills in extreme cold, mountains and skiing, with the aim of creating a ski warfare division. In her book, *Looking Forwards, James Riddell's Adventurous Life on and off the Snow*, Alison, his second wife, recounts how Riddell found himself promoted to Major and running a wartime ski school at the Cedars. Somehow, 500 sets of skis were shipped in, 15 instructors recruited and 2,000 troops were trained on the snow.

The Allies were successful in their campaign, and Riddell, who had already been vice-captain of the British ski team at the 1936 Winter Olympics, went on to have a very adventurous life, as his wife's book details. This included stints as President of the Ski Club of Great Britain, and writing books on skiing, including one of the first guidebooks, *Ski Holidays in the Alps*. The Cedars is still used for military training but now for troops from Lebanon's own army.

NIGHT RUN, SHEMSHAK

IRAN

Along with the extreme friendliness of the people, one of the most noticeable things about Iran is that it has really big mountains. The Alborz range, which forms an impressive snow-capped backdrop to the capital Tehran, includes Mount Damavand, the country's highest at 5,610 metres (18,406 feet). This is about 800 metres (2,624 feet) taller than Mont Blanc, and the Alborz is just one of several mountain ranges in the country, along with about 30 ski areas – true, most are fairly small, but they're there.

Shemshak, located a little over 50 kilometres (31 miles) north-east of Tehran and one of the country's first to open in the late 1950s, holds cult status for skiers and boarders. It's little changed since it opened, and it's a nightmare to reach at the weekend due to traffic (the weekend in Iran is Thursday and Friday), but it's famed for having the country's steepest runs, as well as sublime freeriding terrain when Iran's famously fluffy light powder is at its best – typically in January and February.

There are two aged double chairlifts (one with fetching yellow towers and complementary-coloured orangey-red chairs) and a handful of drag lifts, which together still qualify it as one of Iran's three largest ski areas. It's well above the treeline and the ski slopes are on the open mountain face, which is essentially one huge exposed area, the top of which is reached by both chairlifts.

Iranian ski areas aren't big on piste maps, but two of Shemshak's six runs are officially classified as blacks, one

---

recognised in 1986 by the International Ski Federation (FIS) as able to host officially sanctioned ski competitions. The steepest terrain is at the top of the mountain, where the two chairlifts more or less converge.

But one of the most surreal parts of skiing in Iran is skiing at night. That's possible on the lower 950 metres (3,117 feet) of the slope on the western side. The aged lighting provides an ethereal yellow glow as you float through the powder snow. It's open between 6 and 10pm on Monday to Thursday evenings.

The slopes are largely north-facing, good news for snowfall volumes and snow quality, and average about 5 metres (16 feet) a year. Iran's two other largest resorts, Dizin and Darbandsar, are also nearby, so this is very much the epicentre of Iranian skiing.

The first skiers in Iran are believed to have been German engineers who were there in the early 1930s helping to build railways, but having spotted the big snowy mountains, decided to bring their skis with them and do some touring. By the end of the decade, Iranian students were returning from Europe with skiing skills they'd picked up and were instructing Iranian carpenters on how to build skis.

The Iranian love of skiing continued through the mid-twentieth century with local ski clubs forming. They were joined on the slopes by Western soldiers around World War II, and the first lifts were erected in 1951. The developing Iranian ski scene was then turbo-charged by the last Shah of Iran, Mohammas Reza Pahlavi, a man who by all accounts had an exceptionally strong sense of self-belief, including in his own skiing abilities. He spent some of his vast wealth on a chalet in St. Moritz, holidaying in Sun Valley and building what's generally regarded as the

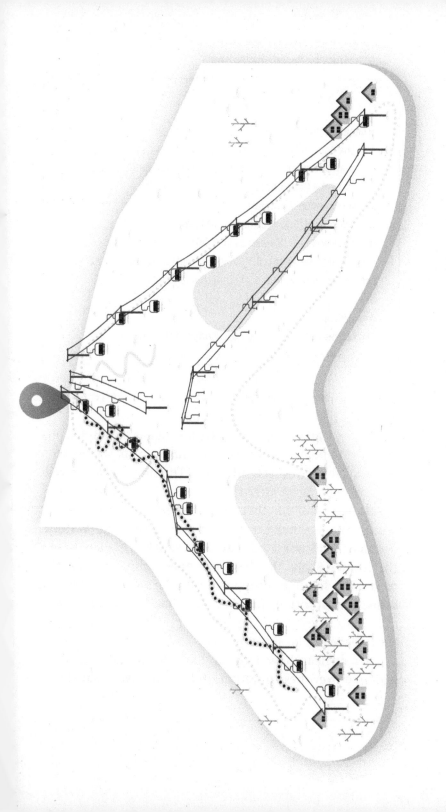

FACT FILE

IN SHORT If Western media is correct, Iran's ski slopes are where the country's youth can escape the scrutiny of the regime and genders can mix. In any case, winter sports long pre-date the Revolution.

DIFFICULTY OF RUN Moderate

VERTICAL OF RUN 500 metres (1,640 feet)

LENGTH OF RUN 1.6 kilometres (1 mile)

SKI AREA ALTITUDE RANGE 2,550–3,050 metres (8,366–10,007 feet)

RESORT AREA DIMENSIONS 15 kilometres (9 miles)

LIFTS 5

WEB skicomplex.ir

GETTING THERE Air to Tehran, 66 kilometres (41 miles)

country's best resort, Dizin, which was half completed when his regime was overthrown.

Today, Iran's relationship with skiing is a complex one and highlights the strengths and flaws in its society in a way that few other activities can. The first challenge religious leaders faced after their success in the 1979 Islamic Revolution was whether skiing should be tolerated at all. On the one hand, the sport was considered Western, decadent, and was of course very closely associated with the former Shah. On the other hand, going up into the mountains felt like getting closer to the divine, potentially something spiritual. Just because snow sports are essentially purely joyful (on a good day, at least), did that mean they needed to be sinful per se?

It's unclear how long or how much the ayatollahs agonised over these questions, but it's believed that skiing was initially banned in the early 1980s before the lifts started turning again reportedly in the middle of the decade and skiers returned.

The next question was should men and women be allowed to ski together? Under the most dogmatic interpretations of religious law, perhaps not. Having fun together could again result in something sinful. Measures taken to enforce these restrictions vary a lot. Many skiers visiting the country say they don't notice any such gender segregation, while journalists working for some right-leaning newspapers in Europe and North America gleefully belittle seemingly farcical attempts to separate the sexes.

The rules reportedly include women being required to cover themselves from head to toe (actually that's fairly straightforward when skiing), having to ride women-only lifts (unless with a close male relative) or skiing on runs again segregated by gender. The lighter side is that the rules need to be enforced by a kind of religious-ethics police and the joke is that they generally don't know how to ski.

At the time of writing, the general direction in Iran is towards a more open-minded view of the world, and that's been reflected in upgrades to old ski areas and even the creation of small new ones in the provinces for the first time since the Revolution more than four decades ago. Unlike a handful of ski areas in the USA, all the ski centres in Iran welcome snowboarders.

THE SKI RUN, MALAM JABBA

PAKISTAN

Ski resorts around the world have faced many challenges over the past century: ski areas have been lost to volcanic eruptions, climate change, war and (most commonly) the whims of changing public demand. In Pakistan, the threat to the country's only real commercial ski area has come on two fronts: political and religious. As a result of one or both of these, it has operated for less than 20 years in the 60 years since it was conceived. But when it can open, it's exceptionally popular.

There's only one official ski run at Malam Jabba, located in the country's spectacular Karakoram mountain range, so the piste map is fairly straightforward. To ski it you need to first board the double chairlift that was officially opened by former cricket star and future Prime Minister, Imran Khan, in 2016. Ascend its 630-metre (2,067-feet) length, as Khan did, turn right as you get off and, well, ski back down.

It would probably be rated a blue run in Europe or North America: straight, nice and wide, and treelined. Actually, much of its length has safety netting on either side so there are no distractions to lure you off the slope. It's a very satisfying descent and unlikely to be crowded as few people are here to ski. Most are content to play in the snow, perhaps do a little sledging and ride the zip wire.

The snow is usually good in midwinter, and the resort averages 3 metres (10 feet) of snowfall annually. You can easily make a day of skiing laps while marvelling at the fact you're one of the few people to have skied in Pakistan.

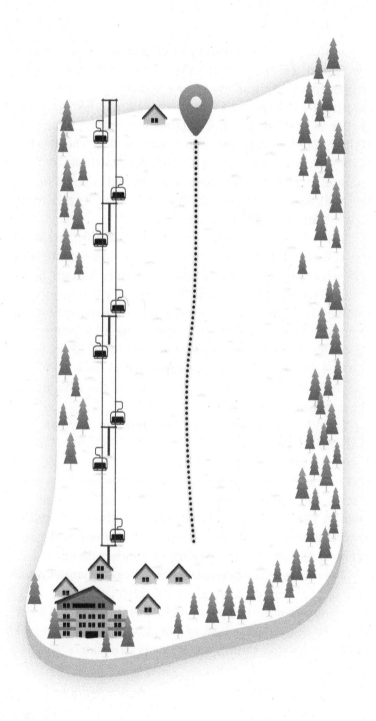

Austria has a long history of helping countries around the world establish their ski areas, and that's what happened in Pakistan in the early 1960s. The country's perpetual rival India had created ski areas just over the border in Kashmir (territory claimed by Pakistan and constantly fought over), including what is now the world's highest full ski area at Gulmarg. Pakistan has its own share of very high mountains (the second highest in the world at 8,611 metres/28,251 feet, K2, is on its territory), so why not have ski areas here as well?

Swat Valley is one of the most beautiful areas in the country, full of lush valleys, green forested hillsides and white snow-capped mountains. Before Malam Jabba opened, there were two Buddhist stupas (structures containing sacred relics that are used as a place of meditation) and six monasteries scattered around the area, suggesting that it has been inhabited for over 2,000 years. Sixty years ago, the Austrian Ambassador suggested to his good friend The Wāli of Swat, the traditional ruler of the area, that a ski resort might be built.

Completing the ski resort took another 25 years. The Wāli gifted the land to the state in 1969 and Austria donated a lot of equipment, including a chairlift and skis and boots for rental. Adding a comfortable hotel and the rest of the resort infrastructure meant it was ready to open in 1988 – except it didn't. Instead, disputes between local landowners and the Pakistan government broke out, delaying Malam Jabba's opening by another decade.

The resort finally opened shortly before the millennium and nearly four decades after its conception. The early years were promising. Malam Jabba was thronged with visitors keen to escape the heat of Islamabad. Many locals took to skiing and the country's most successful skiers began to

---

FACT FILE

IN SHORT Pakistan has perhaps had to fight harder than any other country to be able to offer skiing, even fighting the Taliban to reclaim the slopes and lift; it's time to offer thanks.

DIFFICULTY OF RUN Moderate

VERTICAL OF RUN 201 metres (659 feet)

LENGTH OF RUN 800 metres (2,624 feet)

SKI AREA ALTITUDE RANGE 2,469–2,804 metres (8,100–9,200 feet)

RESORT AREA DIMENSIONS 1 kilometre (0.6 miles)

RUNS 2

LIFTS 2

WEB samsonsgroupco.com

GETTING THERE Air to Saidu Sharif, 51 kilometres (32 miles)

---

win international competitions with some chosen to represent Pakistan at upcoming Winter Olympics.

Things took a sad turn in 2007 when the Taliban stormed into the Swat Valley. Besides a campaign of oppression and murder, they are reported to have initially used the ski resort as their headquarters before burning down the hotel and destroying the ski lift. Their view was that skiing was an 'un-Islamic activity', as had been the case in the early years after Iran's 1979 revolution, but the religious leaders there later decided that skiing could be enjoyed 'to the glory of God' (see Night Run page 205).

The Taliban were driven out in 2009 but it was to be another five years before the Pakistan government brought in a private company to rebuild the resort, and two more before Malam Jabba reopened. In the years since, it has had more periods of closure, but this time due to disputes over revenue share between the centre's operators and local government.

Skiing has had a messy and at times very dark history in Pakistan, perhaps more than any other country, but the future is hopefully brighter. Besides the resurrection of Malam Jabba, other ski areas are being created, including Naltar, previously operated for the Pakistan Air Force. Now open to the public it boasts a new chairlift, this time donated by the Swiss ski resort of Villars. An indoor snow centre has also opened recently in Karachi, the most populous city in the country.

The incredible mountains of Pakistan are also coming into focus as more extreme skiers tackle the world's highest mountains, previously considered impossible slopes. Laila Peak (6,096 metres/ 20,000 feet) in the Hushe Valley by the Gondogoro glacier has become a magnet for the world's greatest ski mountaineers, who consider the slope from its summit, which descends at a nearly constant angle of 45 degrees for more than 1,500 vertical metres (4,921 feet), among the most perfect natural runs on earth. French skiers Carole Chambaret, Tiphaine Duperier and Boris Langenstein, ski instructors and mountain guides from Val d'Isère, claimed to be the first to ski it in full in 2018.

That same year also saw the first successful descent from the summit of K2 on skis, nearly two decades after the first attempt. The world's second-highest peak is considered a greater challenge than slightly higher Everest, both to ascend and to ski down, but Polish ski-mountaineer Andrzej Bargiel was successful on his second attempt. Like Malam Jabba and Laila Peak, K2 is in the Karakoram range.

ROCK, YANQING

CHINA

China's rise to fame as a global superpower of winter sports has been meteoric. From a near-standing start at the turn of the twenty-first century, more than 700 ski areas have popped up across the country and tens of millions of Chinese people have given skiing or snowboarding a go. They've been egged on by President Xi Jinping who, in 2015, set a target of 300 million of his country's people trying winter sports before the start of the 2022 Games (they hit 346 million by the start of the Olympics). That's more than the skiing population of the rest of the world combined.

The rapid creation of all these ski areas has not been without its challenges. Although China is big, the majority of its population live in the flatter, sub-tropical parts of the country. True it has the Himalayas, but they're distant, sparsely populated and too high for most Chinese people just looking for a nursery slope. So the bulk of the destination ski resort development, including the 2022 Winter Olympic venue, is in the north-east of the country, a region known for its bitingly cold winters, but not so much for mountains or abundant snowfall.

But this is China, where all natural challenges are overcome. More than 30 indoor snow centres have popped up across the country, including the world's three largest yet, each with close to a kilometre (0.6 miles) of indoor snow slopes and thronging with volumes of keen novice skiers the West can only dream of.

The 2022 Winter Olympics were certainly a driving force for the growth of winter sports in the country, and now that the games are disappearing in the rear-view mirror it will be interesting to see if the momentum continues. Many of the hundreds of ski areas that have popped up are simple affairs with a couple of small lifts and a snowmaking machine that could disappear just as quickly. There's currently not many big resorts for newly snow-addicted skiers to progress on to, but that is changing quickly, and the ski centres created for the Games are the pièce de résistance.

The planet's newest Olympic downhill, christened simply 'Rock', is one of the steepest racecourses in the world, with four extra-steep sections where the world's best racers got airborne for up to 44 metres (144 feet) at a time during the 2022 Games. With speeds hitting 137 kmh (85 mph), they actually spent about 10 per cent of the race in the air.

Like all things Chinese skiing, the Yanqing National Alpine Ski Centre is very new, opening in late 2019, just as the global coronavirus pandemic began. As a result, it was the first racecourse in modern times that the competing ski racers had not skied before they arrived in late February 2022. It was created purely for the Olympics but has now become a ski resort.

Located on Xiaohaituo Mountain, the terrain has been described as the most complex to design a course on in Winter Olympic history. However, nine fast lifts from the world's leading manufacturer Doppelmayr, more than half of them gondolas, make getting around the slopes quick and comfortable. In an unusual resort configuration, these gondolas take you through a narrow valley from the resort to the ski slopes. After climbing around 1,100 vertical

metres (3,608 feet) the lifts arrive at a huge kite-shaped wooden building at the top of the slopes from where the downhill racecourse begins.

The run follows the undulating natural terrain of the mountainside. There are a hundred metres (328 feet) or so of open mountainside and splendid views of the forest and valleys below, before, almost immediately it seems, you're within the treeline. Race viewers quickly became familiar with the course sections – Cyclone, The Saddle Jump, Silk Road, the huge Sugar Jump, and then the flat and narrow Canyon to the base. Taken at full speed it's a fast, technical course, but skiing at your own pace it's a really pleasant run for a recreational skier of moderate ability or above.

The main focus of Western media coverage at the Olympics was that there was no natural snow cover at Yanqing. Instead, European snow machines had made ribbons of white down the brown slopes, which most of the athletes said they actually rather liked. Some pointed out that most racecourses around the world are covered with machine-made snow these days anyway, and that having consistent low temperatures was the real positive.

A high-speed railway line from Beijing, which opened a year or so before the Games, sees trains reach 350 kmh (217 mph) and means the 80 kilometres (50 miles) from Beijing to the ski resort can be covered in about half an hour.

Since the 1988 Winter Olympics, courses, including this one, have been designed by the great Swiss racer Bernhard Russi from Andermatt. We can tie Russi, who won gold himself in the downhill at the 1972 Olympics in Sapporo, Japan, to two other runs in this book. In 1969, just after winning a place on the Swiss team on the newly

FACT FILE

IN SHORT The 2022 Winter Olympic downhill was the first in the Games' history not to have been raced before the Olympics themselves. Built new for 2022, planned test events were cancelled due to the pandemic.

DIFFICULTY OF RUN Moderate–Difficult

VERTICAL OF RUN 890 metres (2,920 feet)

LENGTH OF RUN 4 kilometres (2.5 miles)

SKI AREA ALTITUDE RANGE 1,200–2,190 metres (3,937–7,185 feet)

RESORT AREA DIMENSIONS 25 kilometres (16 miles)

LIFTS 9

WEB beijing2022.cn

GETTING THERE Rail to Yanqing, 19 kilometres (12 miles); or Air to Beijing, 90 kilometres (56 miles)

established World Cup circuit, Russi suffered a fractured cervical vertebra while working as a stuntman on the Bond movie *On Her Majesty's Secret Service* (see Piste 10, page 104). Then, in the 1976 Winter Games, Russi was the man Klammer (see Klammer's Run, page 152) beat into silver in one of the greatest Olympic downhills of all time.

Alas, the Winter Olympics have not been a great advertisement for environmentally friendly skiing in recent decades. The most recent Games, 2022 in China and 2018 in South Korea, saw downhill courses created in pristine environments, cutting through what was supposed to have been protected national parkland. A key issue was that downhill courses must have at least an 800-metre (2,624-feet) vertical, and neither country had anything that quite met the criteria.

In China's case, there was initially a huge online outcry when the location of the course was announced, but this was quickly silenced and, allegedly, its previously environmentally protected status quietly removed. China has been keen to report that although a bit of nature reserve was lost to the ski slope, they've expanded it by far more elsewhere and bio-diversity has increased.

In Korea's case, the location required the felling of ancient trees to create the course, again causing outrage. Olympic organisers agreed to restore the land after the Games and remove a brand-new, multi-million-dollar gondola lift installed especially for it. Legal battles to reverse that requirement have been going on ever since, but at the time of writing the court decided that the agreement must be adhered to and the site restored at a much greater cost than its construction.

Hopefully for the second century of the Winter Olympics, projects that require any damage to the natural environment will no longer be successful when bidding to host future Games.

RUN 1, MASIK PASS

NORTH KOREA

North Korea's aspiration to be a winter sports tourism destination made world headlines in 2014. In part the West wanted to belittle Kim Jong-un's idea of creating a ski resort from scratch in less than a year, but they also wanted to express righteous indignation that he had somehow managed to secure decent lifts, snowmaking machinery and other bits of ski kit despite UN sanctions.

The construction of Masik Pass, or 'Masikryong' in Korean, was announced as a 'giant patriotic work' by Kim Jong-un and even generated a slogan, and indeed a whole way of thinking for North Koreans: 'Masikryong speed'. It doesn't refer to how fast you ski down the slopes, but that you perform diligently, efficiently, speedily in every aspect of your life.

The belief that Masikryong was constructed by a near-starving slave labour army or by inspired patriots depends on whether you're reading Western or North Korean views on the construction. What both sides do agree on, if rather grudgingly on the Western side, is that the quality of skiing is pretty good. Early cynical reports that the resort would only be used by the military and party elite, or that the nine-storey hotel complex that went up so fast could collapse, have so far proved unfounded.

It appears the young leader of the reclusive state has been keen on skiing from childhood, having spent some years at private schools in Switzerland. The Northern Korean government doesn't exactly want to advertise that its future leaders may have been educated in Switzerland.

However, the theory is that two North Korean kids attending Swiss private schools in the late 1990s, purporting to be the children of diplomats, were actually Kim Jong-un and his older brother Kim Jong-chul. South Korea's *Hankook Ilbo* newspaper reported in 2009, as the then 26-year-old Kim Jong-un emerged from international obscurity to be unveiled as the country's future leader, that he enjoyed skiing and basketball.

In fact Kim Jong-un's Masik Pass ski area that grabbed the world's attention was not the first to be built in North Korea. Kim's father Kim Jong-il (another fan of all things Swiss, including fondue) had installed a double chairlift, rumoured to have been donated by a Swiss ski resort in a goodwill gesture in the era before sanctions, on Mount Paektu in Ryanggang Province. Called Begaebong, the world didn't notice it and instead declared Masik Pass the country's first (built as UN sanctions due to North Korea's nuclear missile programme were starting to bite), with colourful headlines such as 'War & Piste'. Several more North Korean ski areas, perhaps not so impressive in scale, have been built since.

Run number 1 (of nine) is the longest and gentlest of Masik Pass's runs, descending the full 592-metre (1,942 feet) vertical of the resort and following the ski area's boundary for around 5 kilometres (3 miles). Along with shorter, steeper runs 6, 7, 8 and 9, run 1 begins up at Taehwa Peak, reached via an elderly four-seat gondola lift which was installed a few years after the resort opened in 2014, replacing a 30-year-old chairlift imported (indirectly) from Austria.

At the top of Taehwa there's a mountain restaurant from which you can take in some of the best scenic views of North Korea. The view extends as far as the coastal city

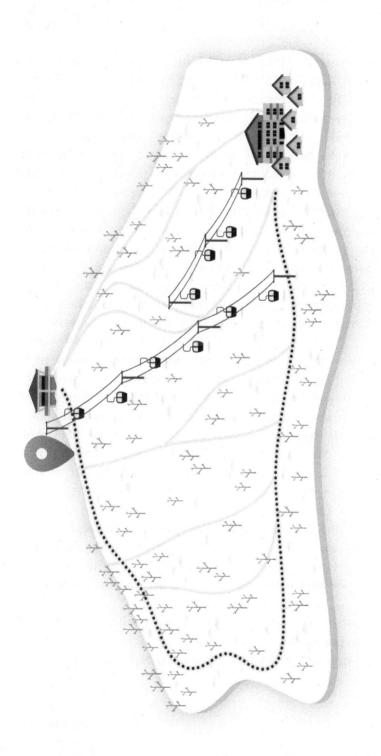

of Wonsan, 20 kilometres (13 miles) away, and out over the Sea of Japan (or the East Sea of Korea as the locals know it). Masik Pass means 'horse resting place', and as you gaze out over this remote area you can appreciate why horses needed a rest if they were trying to travel across it.

Alas, as is the case for much of the eastern Asian mainland, including North Korea's large and currently ski-obsessed neighbour China, big dumps of snow are relatively rare. Instead, cold, dry air usually moves across the region from the west, scoops up moisture when it reaches the Sea of Japan/East Sea of Korea, then famously dumps powder in abundance when the air rises and cools again as it hits Japan's mountains. It's unknown if this quirk of geographic and meteorological fate in Japan's favour is a further cause of irritation between the Asian neighbours. But unless you get lucky and arrive in North Korea after a rare natural powder dump, you are most likely to be skiing on a mixture of the thin natural snow cover, well preserved by the normally double-digit sub-zero temperatures, topped up with machine-made snow. It should provide you with a satisfying top-to-bottom high-speed cruise down the slopes, and the fact that you are skiing in North Korea at all surely adds to the satisfaction of completing this run. Probably followed by the other eight runs in the next hour or so.

Who does ski Masik Pass? Well, it depends which version you choose to believe. Western media claim that it is only the country's elite who are allowed on the slopes. And it does appear that the cost of a lift pass, let alone a stay in the hotel there, is way beyond the spending power of most of the country's population. North Korea, however, insists that the centre is open to all. This difference in perception was crucial in arguments over whether Western

FACT FILE

IN SHORT Kim Jong-un is reported to have loved skiing since his (alleged) time at a Swiss finishing school. His ski resort posed the bigger question as to whether skiing is a luxury sport when it came to sanctions.

DIFFICULTY OF RUN Easy

VERTICAL OF RUN 692 metres (2,270 feet)

LENGTH OF RUN 4.8 kilometres (3 miles)

SKI AREA ALTITUDE RANGE 768–1,360 metres (2,520–4,460 feet)

RESORT AREA DIMENSIONS 17 kilometres (11 miles)

RUNS 9

LIFTS 7

WEB tourismdprk.gov.kp

GETTING THERE Rail to Wŏnsan, 46 kilometres (29 miles); or Air to Wŏnsan, 50 kilometres (31 miles)

companies should supply the equipment the resort needed when it was built. At the time, UN sanctions banned the sale of 'luxury sporting goods', which some Western governments interpreted as meaning 'ski gear when it's for the elite' and cancelled deals. Meanwhile, other nations such as China, itself in the process of building new ski resorts, took the North Korean position that skiing was good for the mental and physical health of the nation and shouldn't be penalised. In the end, Chinese brokers bought the equipment from Europe and sold it on to North Korea. Problem solved.

As the years have passed since Masik Pass was completed in 2014, it appears that the skiers there are a mix of well-heeled North Koreans, adventure-seeking Westerners, and quite a large number of Chinese, who say that the ski quality is higher and costs less than at many of their local hills.

One of Kim Jong-un's ambitions in building Masik Pass was to, somehow, jointly host the 2018 Winter Olympics awarded to its southern neighbour. Alas that never happened, but there were a few rare moments of comradery as for the first time a joint North and South Korean team competed in one event, and the divided nation's teams entered together under a Korean Unification Flag during the opening ceremony.

RAINBOW 1, YONGPYONG

SOUTH KOREA

South Korea is one of those countries where it's surprising for many that there is any skiing at all. It came as an even bigger surprise when the country was awarded the 2018 Winter Olympics. However, the South Koreans had repeatedly bid to host the Olympics, just losing out to Canada's Vancouver bid in 2010 and again to Sochi in Russia in 2014, before finally winning four years later. Everybody loves a trier.

There are actually around 15 ski areas in South Korea, most of the larger ones in the Taebaek Mountains in the province of Gangwon-do, also the location of PyeongChang, the Olympic host region. Yongpyong (which translates to 'Dragon Valley') is located here and is the largest and oldest ski resort in Korea, although that's still not very old. It hosted the slalom and giant slalom events at the 2018 Olympics and was being considered for the Olympic downhill. They planned to build a platform at the top of the slopes to increase the vertical to the minimum for an Olympic downhill (otherwise it's about 60 vertical metres (197 feet) short). In the end the idea was abandoned in favour of (controversially) building on a virgin site (see Rock, page 215).

Yongpyong offers terrain for all abilities, when most Korean areas focus on a particular market sector. The slopes on the three mountains above the resort have been divided into four zones christened the Rainbow, Gold, Red and Silver zones. The Rainbow lifts and runs are located on Dragon Mountain, the highest point of the whole ski area at 1,458 metres (4,783 feet) and were previously known as the 'Dragon Zone', which is perhaps a more impressive-sounding title.

Yongpyong's ski area layout is a little unusual. The Rainbow group of four black-graded runs is way off to the right of the area (looking up at the mountain) and accessed by a 3.7-kilometre (2.3-mile) long gondola, which takes about 20 minutes to make the ascent. From the top of the gondola there are not the usual multiple routes back down to the base, just the one very, very long easy run (Rainbow Paradise, 5.6 kilometres/3.5 miles in length and Korea's second-longest piste). So once you've finished skiing the black runs you will need to return to the top of the gondola via a chairlift and take the Rainbow Paradise run (or gondola) all the way back down.

The world's best skiers were here in February 2018 when the Olympic giant slalom race was staged on Rainbow I, the longest of the four black runs in the Rainbow sector at 1,630 metres (5,348 feet). This would probably be a red run in the Alps, a single black diamond in North America; wide and smooth, it is simply steeper than most of the rest of the runs, dropping 410 vertical metres (1,345 feet) over its length with an average gradient of 34.4 per cent. The trail cuts through the thick forest but high nets line either side so there's no chance of getting into the trees. It's usually best to enjoy a high-speed descent, imagining you're an Olympian, a delusion helped by the fact that some large Olympic rings come into view as you near the base. It's just the cheering crowds that are missing.

The other three Rainbow runs are of similar stature and all worth a run or two. Rainbow II is the second drop off to the right after Rainbow I and descends just below the chairlift. This was also featured in the 2018 Olympics, with

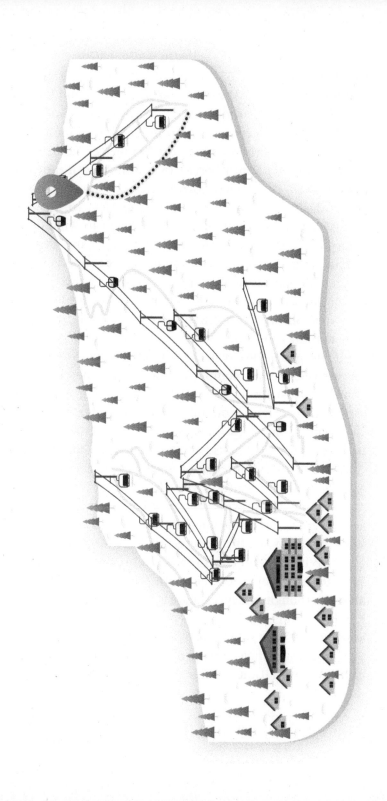

the slalom races staged on it. It's about one degree steeper. Rainbow III is under the chair line and the second longest of the rainbows, 100 metres (328 feet) shorter than I and has the option of a cut-through from Rainbow II for a bit of variety. Run IV is the shortest, just 635 metres (2,083 feet).

When to ski South Korea? In common with much of eastern Asia, the coldest weather tends to run a month or so ahead of Europe and North America, so the first half of winter is usually best; things begin to wind down from mid-February and the snow can be slushy. Even in a good year, South Korea's mountains do not get that much snow; this is not a place with a high chance of finding powder. Annual average snowfall totals are less than 2 metres (6.5 feet), but there's the predictable arsenal of snowmaking cannons.

If you spend the day in the Rainbow section you'll want to visit the summit complex, which is also popular with non-skiers just up for the gondola ride. Along with great views out over the mountains and the obligatory coffee shop, you'll find both a Korean restaurant and a slightly surreal Alpine steakhouse in a Swiss-themed building.

Skiing, at least in terms of organised ski areas, arrived a little later in South Korea than other major skiing nations but has proved very popular in recent decades, and ski areas can be open from early morning until late at night. Much of Yongpyong's terrain is floodlit and open to 10pm. With an 8am start, that's double the length of the average ski day in Europe or North America. Korean nights are cold, though. Indeed, ski areas are so popular that one, Konjiam, limits lift ticket sales to 7,000 people a day so you know you'll have some space on the slopes.

Crowding can be an issue on the long slope back to the base after your time on the Paradise run. Lots of novice

FACT FILE

IN SHORT The 2018 Olympic giant slalom slope is one of the best-known runs in South Korea, its reputation bolstered by its long access gondola taking centre-stage in one of the country's most popular TV series.

DIFFICULTY OF RUN Moderate

VERTICAL OF RUN 500 metres (1,640 feet)

LENGTH OF RUN 1.6 kilometres (1 mile)

SKI AREA ALTITUDE RANGE 700–1,438 metres (2,297–4,718 feet)

RESORT AREA DIMENSIONS 24 kilometres (15 miles)

RUNS 28

LIFTS 14

WEB yongpyong.co.kr

GETTING THERE Rail to Jinbu, 14 kilometres (9 miles); or Air to Wŏnju, 72 kilometres (45 miles)

skiers ride the gondola up to spend hours trundling down. The run is narrow in places where it follows a ridge, and there are high permanent fences on each side of the slope for its entire length. Once you set off there's nothing to do but carry on, avoiding all the slower skiers and boarders in your path. Pistes do start to branch off eventually, after about 4 kilometres (2.5 miles).

I have mentioned famous Bond and The Beatles' film associations elsewhere in this book, but for avid fans of Korean dramas, the gondola ride up to Dragon Peak is the very place where Shin (Gong Yoo) and Eun-Tak (Kim Go-eun) share some of their most romantic moments in the hit TV series *Goblin: The Lonely and Great God*.

RIESEN SLALOM, HAPPO-ONE

JAPAN

Over the past few decades, Japan has become famous for its exceptional snow conditions. Traditionally, Japan hasn't celebrated its remarkable volumes of super-light, 'snorkel-deep' powder snow. In fact, heading off the groomed runs was, and in many areas still is, illegal, due to the perceived risk of danger to the skier/boarder and those who might have to go and rescue them.

The northern island of Hokkaido, particularly resorts like Niseko, have enjoyed a meteoric rise to ski world fame, but in truth most of Japan's 500 or so ski areas have plenty of powder to offer. Niseko was one of the first to allow access to the untouched powder, which typically totals more than 10 metres (33 feet) each winter, via back country gates into approved areas considered generally avalanche-safe.

Other ski areas, seeing international investment flow into an economy that was decimated by the collapse of the country's so-called 'bubble economy' more than three decades ago, are trying to follow suit. But despite that world-renowned powder, most Japanese skiers tend to stick to the groomed runs, which is why I've done the same.

Hakuba, one of Japan's great ski regions and a host venue at the 1998 Nagano Winter Olympics, contains some of the country's biggest mountains, spectacular scenery and deepest snow. It's also home to a densely packed collection of ski areas including Happo-One, where the season usually lasts well into May. There are nine separate ski

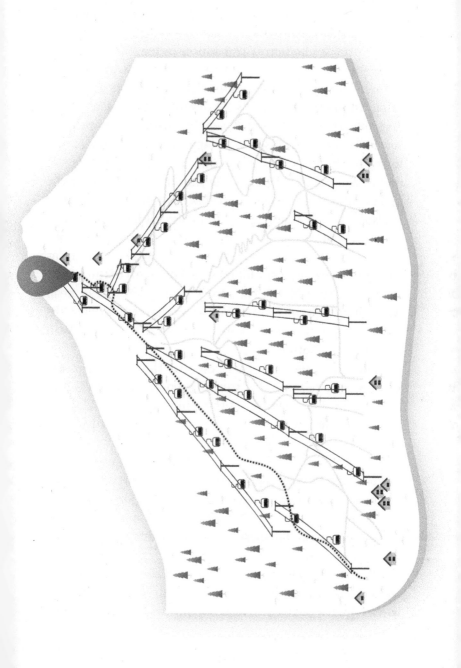

centres in the Hakuba Valley, which together operate more than 130 lifts serving more than 200 ski runs.

At over 4 kilometres (2.5 miles) in length, the Riesen Slalom at Happo-One is built to the standard of an international racecourse, complete with an average 20-degree pitch, in places as steep as 30 degrees. The run has been arguably the most famous run in Japan for more than seven decades. Accessed by Happo's Adam gondola followed by the successive Alpen and Grat quad chairlifts, it's one of the longest runs on the mountain and one of the biggest lift-served vertical descents possible in the country. It also serves as a homage to all dedicated Japanese skiers.

Once you reach the top of the lifts, simply point your boards downhill and let rip, always staying skier's right as the run's line of descent follows the boundary of the resort. Ignore the turnoff left back to the base and instead head down alongside the Nakiyama double chair No. 1 ('pair lift' to the Japanese), staying skier's left via the Nakiyama Wall and on to the bottom.

The run is usually at its best first thing in the morning, not only because it is freshly groomed and you'll beat the crowds, but with its south-facing aspect the morning sunlight illuminates a fabulous descent with stupendous views out over Hakuba.

The Riesen Slalom (it means 'giant slalom') was created more than 75 years ago thanks to the efforts of skiing enthusiast Fukuoka Takayuki, whose day job was teaching German and PE at Hosei University. Takayuki wanted to create a great Japanese ski run capable of staging an international ski race that could rival and even surpass those that were beginning to appear in the European Alps. He had already made a name for himself as a pioneer of winter sports technique instruction in Japan and, having

studied different methods being taught at the time in
Europe and North America, had published his own book of
instruction based on what he considered the best practice.

Having moved to the Hakuba region in the late 1930s,
Takayuki convinced the local authorities of the potential
for winter sports tourism immediately after the conclusion
of World War II. He identified Happo-One as the location
for his Riesen Slalom course and work was completed by
1946.

Takayuki's dream was realised the following year
with the first Happo-One Riesen Slalom competition held
in 1947. At the time there were no ski lifts so the race
began with an ascent of more than 1,000 vertical metres
(3,281 feet) to reach the start of the course, adding to
the challenge. It's not recorded how long it took the first
winner to get up to the start line, but it took him 5 minutes

29 seconds to get down. Neither is it recorded what the winner's name was. Things got much easier in 1954 when the first lift, Nakiyama, was installed.

At 4.5 kilometres (2.8 miles) long with 1,030 metres (3,379 feet) of vertical, the run far surpasses the dimensions required by the International Ski Federation (FIS) and all of the world's best known World Cup descents – including the longest, Switzerland's 4.48-kilometre (2.78-mile) Lauberhorn (page 99). It remains one of the longest runs of any kind in Japan and the vertical drop among the country's 10 greatest.

Takayuki died in 1981 but his racing dream continues to be a major success. Happo-One was the venue for the men's and women's Olympic downhill and super-G races at the Nagano Olympics, staged four decades after Takayuki created his run. The famous Austrian racer Herman 'The Herminator' Maier won the super-G race at Happo-One, as well as 'doing the double' by winning the more technical giant slalom race staged at Shiga Kogen. That was perhaps not the result Mr Takayuki envisaged when he sought to inspire Japanese racers, but hopefully he'd still be happy.

More than 75 years later, the race he founded in 1947 continues to be staged each winter and is a big draw for both local amateurs and more serious international racers. There are different racing categories divided by age and gender, and everyone who competes receives an oval-shaped badge, coloured black, blue or red depending on how close they got to the winner.

INTERNATIONAL, FALLS CREEK

AUSTRALIA

The world's best ski racers love to head to the southern hemisphere to train between June and October, but these days races outside of the World Cup tour attracting the world's best are somewhat rare. International events do take place in the Andes and New Zealand in late August or early September, but they are usually locally organised contests that the world's elite tend to use for race training ahead of the tour proper, which begins each northern hemisphere autumn. It runs between October and March, starting on Alpine glaciers just as the southern hemisphere's season ends.

In the pioneering years of international ski racing, after the initial competitions in the Alps and before the World Cup tour got underway in the late 1960s, races were staged in developing ski resorts all over the planet. One of these, in the Australian resort of Falls Creek in north-eastern Victoria, was such a big deal that the resort built a bridge over its access road so that the racecourse, today known as the International, could continue down for the full 450 vertical metres (1,476 feet) required by regulations of the day. That's about 170 vertical metres (557 feet) longer than the slope today.

That descent begins with the blue-graded Skyline, which runs just below the exposed ridgeline of Frying Pan Spur, one of more than half-a-dozen runs starting from a spot served by both the Summit quad and a long drag lift. Having followed the ridge with terrain dropping below to skier's right, with much of the resort's main ski area laid out below and the drag lift to the left, the terrain begins to open up as it reaches the treeline. Here Skyline swings right, becoming the Village Run and continuing to the top of the resort base. But at the turn, three black-graded runs drop away to the left, International the middle run. From here the descent straightens out and it's a high-speed carve down.

The bridge built to extend the run was demolished just a few years after the race was staged, but along with the ski run it's commemorated by the International Poma lift. This was constructed in 1969 above the line of the race-course and is still going strong.

For ski lift nerds the International is the longest 'cornered Poma' in the southern hemisphere and is also believed to be the second-fastest drag lift in the southern hemisphere (after fellow Aussie resort Mount Buller's Howqua Poma). However, it's more beloved by young skiers and boarders for the fact that going around the corner at tower nine on the ascent gives enough centrifugal force to help them jump into the air. It's a practice banned by the resort as it frequently causes the lift to derail, spoiling things for everyone, most notably in 2015 when the damage caused was so severe that it took two weeks for the required spare parts to arrive from Europe. Derailment is only one of the challenges the lift has survived over its more than five decades of loyal operation, with another a major bush fire that raged around it in 2003.

The annual opening of 'The Inter', as the lift is lovingly known, relies on snow depth build-up. It's usually the last of Falls Creeks' dozen or so lifts to open and when it does you know the snow is looking good. It didn't open for the first time until 1970, a decade after the race, as '69 wasn't a vintage snow season.

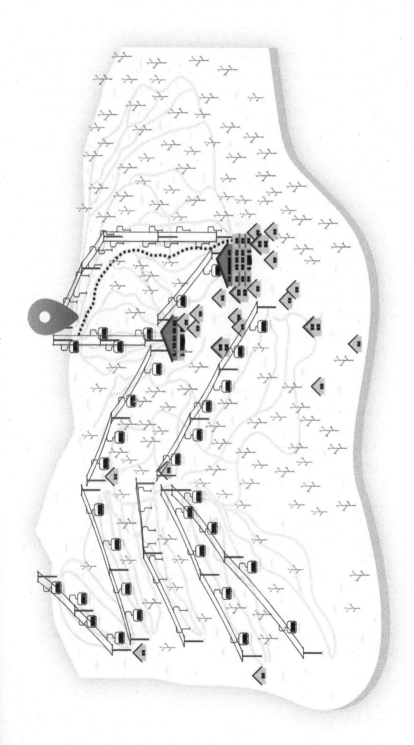

Whether they knew it at the time or not, the race at Falls Creek took place a century after what were, as far as anyone knows, the first downhill ski races anywhere in the world, which took place in Norway, the US and not too far away in Australia. There's been some debate as to where the first-ever ski club was established. Surprisingly, the Kiandra Snow Shoe Club, established in July 1861 in Australia's New South Wales has the strongest case. Alas, little or no documentation has survived to prove anything (due in part to fires over the years), but 1861 is agreed to be when ski clubs were first formalised, and it's all down to Norway. Norwegian miners are credited with bringing skiing to America and Australia in the 1850s during gold rush times. This was a decade or so before Sondre Norheim discovered the Telemark technique that allowed for downhill skiing. Another club, established at what's now one of Norway's leading resorts of Trysil, can also trace its roots to 1861, but a little later in the year.

After decades of disputes through the 1960s, the Kiandra Snow Shoe Club, established by Norwegian miners, was recognised by the International Ski Federation (FIS) in 2011 as the first-ever ski club (2011 was also the 100th anniversary of the FIS and the 150th of the Kiandra Snow Shoe Club). Kiandra 'Ski Carnivals' were held by the club from the early 1860s, and by 1885 there are records of races for children and women. Barbara Yan is the first woman recorded as winning a downhill skiing championship anywhere in the world in 1885, and she won again in 1887.

In 1908 the club staged the first-ever documented downhill ski competition to attract racers from all over the world. The winner was an American, one Charles Menger of Denver, Colorado, a local Aussie was second and a Brit third.

FACT FILE

IN SHORT A run once extended for a rare international race in Australia, now served by one of the most iconic lifts in the southern hemisphere.

DIFFICULTY OF RUN Difficult

VERTICAL OF RUN 278 metres (912 feet)

LENGTH OF RUN 1.2 kilometres (0.75 miles)

SKI AREA ALTITUDE RANGE 1,500–1,780 metres (4921–5840 feet)

RESORT AREA DIMENSIONS 450 hectares (1,112 acres)

RUNS 90

LIFTS 14

WEB fallscreek.com.au

GETTING THERE Air to Albury, 121 kilometres (75 miles)

The idea of building structures to extend racecourses as Falls Creek did with their bridge is still going strong. Verbier used a structure at the top of its speed skiing course to try to break the nearly 255 kmh (158.5 mph) world record, and Grandvalira in Andorra spent €10 million building a 14,000 sq m (150,000 sq ft) structure at the foot of their Avet racecourse before hosting the 2019 World Cup Finals.

ORGAN PIPES, TŪROA

NEW ZEALAND

For those who were not already familiar with the other-worldly grandeur of New Zealand's mountains, the Lord of the Rings film franchise, in 2001, introduced the country's three dozen or so ski fields to the world. Plenty of the country's liftees and ski instructors got some welcome summer income dressing up as Orcs as well.

That global exposure turbo-charged already healthy tourism to New Zealand, and the country's commercial ski fields (there's a distinct difference between those and small centres operated by volunteers and ski clubs) have gone from strength to strength. Whichever ski area you choose, it is hard not to find stunning views and spectacular scenery.

The majority of New Zealand's ski areas are located on the larger but less populated South Island. Winter tends to arrive a little later on the North Island, but this is home to the country's largest resort, on Mount Ruapehu, an active volcano and the island's highest point. It's divided into two separate ski areas, Whakapapa and Tūroa, but under joint management with a single lift ticket valid for both.

Like almost all ski areas on volcanoes the world over, the terrain at Tūroa gets steeper the higher up the mountain you go. Unlike most volcanoes, the ski area also has its best chairlift, the high-speed six-seater High Noon Express chair, to whisk you up to the highest lift-served point in New Zealand at around 2,290 metres (7,513 feet). This opens up the country's biggest lift-served vertical (722 metres/2,369 feet) in the process.

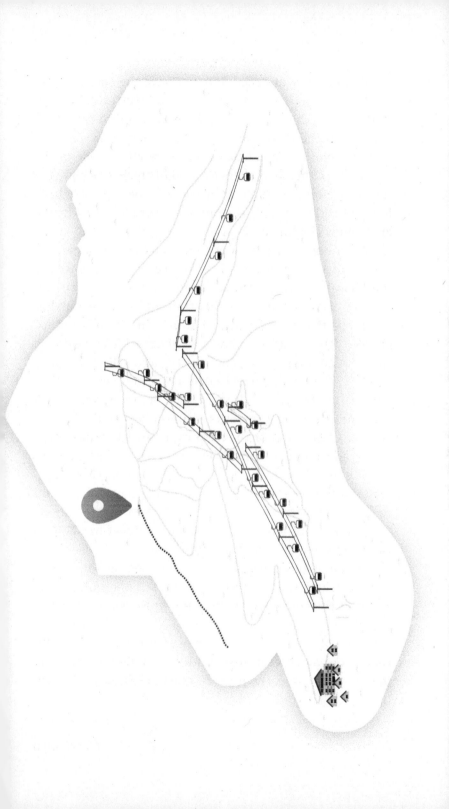

If conditions are good and you have the stamina, you can hike on up another 470 or so vertical metres (1,542 feet) to the top of the mountain and look down into the crater lake. From there you can ski back down to Tūroa's slope or head round to Whakapapa on the northern side of the mountain. Otherwise, there's a load of steep, black-graded terrain stretching off along the ski area boundary to both left and right, as well as gentler blue-graded runs in the area below the lift.

Reaching the Organ Pipes chutes takes local knowledge and often some determination. An access trail follows the top boundary line of Tūroa's groomed terrain. Then you actually need to jump off this trail and traverse further landscape that is not groomed at all and often full of ice chunks; it's manageable but a calf-burner! The views are spectacular from up here, but the terrain is of course very volcanic, shaped by ancient lahar and lava flows, so expect natural gullies, quick drops, rocky outcrops and rough halfpipes with some smooth terrain in between.

The Chutes are for the most experienced all-mountain skiers and boarders only. There may be perfect powder, but ice build-up is a high probability too. These east-facing walls are shaded for much of the day and do tend to gather powder stashes better than most other spots on the mountain. There are fabulous natural features here to carve between or bounce over too.

Ruapehu often boasts the longest ski season in the southern hemisphere, and some years is the only centre south of the equator still operating in November, the last month of spring, or 'Snowvember' as they prefer when the lifts are still running. The late season is thanks to the altitude of the highest terrain at both areas. The early opening in late May or early June is machine-assisted though;

FACT FILE

IN SHORT Some of New Zealand's most exciting terrain is located at the ski area with the country's biggest lift served vertical and often the southern hemisphere's longest season.

DIFFICULTY OF RUN Expert

VERTICAL OF RUN 722 metres (2,369 feet)

LENGTH OF RUN 4 kilometres (2.5 miles)

SKI AREA ALTITUDE RANGE 1,623–2,322 metres (5,325–7,618 feet)

RESORT AREA DIMENSIONS 500 hectares (1,236 acres)

RUNS 20 kilometres (13 miles)

LIFTS 8

WEB mtruapehu.com/turoa

GETTING THERE Air to Auckland, 365 kilometres (227 miles)

Whakapapa has a SnowFactory all-weather snowmaking machine that covers a beginner area whatever the ambient temperature. The main season begins about a month later in late June or early July.

Tūroa's fast chairlift and other advances mark major modernisations and improvements since locals in the nearest community of Ohakune decided to build a road up to the future ski area in the early 1950s. The road, 17 kilometres (11 miles) long, was hand-built over more than a decade, eventually being completed in 1963. It climbs up through beautiful native woodland, and among its many claims to fame, it has an elephant buried beneath it. It was to be another 15 years before the first ski lift was installed. Today, Mount Ruapehu continues to go from strength to strength, and more fast chairlifts and a gondola are due to be installed at Tūroa by 2030.

Credits

The following people helped create this book, and I'm very grateful; apologies to anyone missed.

Susie Aust, Frank Baldwin, Janelle Barnard, Nadya Baron, Emma Bebb, Ken Bell, Jacqueline Bommer, Félix Burke, Claire Burnet, Nadine Carle-Edgar, Alex Clarke, Maria Alessandro Damiani, Lindsay Davies, Lynsey Devon, Nicole Dorigo, Dan Evans, Sarah Evans, Chris Exall, Dora Filli, Vanessa Fisher, Daniel Frizzi, Debbie Gabriel, Betony Garner, Sue Heady, Jenny Hodder, Stefanie Irsara, Jem Jayne, Remo Käser, Stephanie and Michael Lehnort, Dominic Killinger, Fiona Liddell Thorne, Maria Löcker, Aaron McCartney, Colin Maclennan, Rupert Mellor, Maria Alessandra Montuori, Anne Morgan, Matt Mosteller, Are Nundal, Carlos Palomero, Jane Parritt, David Pellatt, Céline Perrillon, Adam Ruck, Nick Russill, Madeline Sauser, Anna Schiestl, John Sellers, Tyler Shultz, Richard Sinclair, Emma Soffe, Chad Sokol, Theresa Sommerbichler, Jessica Staley, Rob Stewart, Geoff Sutton, Marion Telsnig, Julia Thomas, Alexander Thorne, Catherine Thorne, Chilly Thorne, Derek Thorne, Nora Thorne, Robert Thorne, Sally Thorne, Samuel Thorne, Lisa Tyrrell, Luisa Uruena, Jürgen Walch, Sarah Watt, Maïté Werder and Arnie Wilson.

Special thanks to this book's editor, Philip Connor, proofreader, Aruna Vasudevan at The Literary Shed, and copy editor, Rachel Malig.